D1706343

Notes for Serials Cataloging

NOTES FOR SERIALS CATALOGING

Second Edition

Revised and Edited by

Beverley Geer
Head Cataloger, Trinity University

and

Beatrice L. Caraway
Serials Cataloger, Trinity University

Foreword by
Regina Romano Reynolds,
Head of the National Serials Data Program,
Library of Congress

First Edition Compiled by
Nancy G. Thomas

and

Rosanna O'Neil

1998
Libraries Unlimited, Inc.
Englewood, Colorado

For my grandmother, Ella Lucille Powell
B.G.

For David, Wilbur, and Bea
B.C.

LIBRARIES UNLIMITED, INC.
P.O. Box 6633
Englewood, CO 80155-6633
1-800-237-6124
www.lu.com

Production Editor: Stephen Haenel
Proofreader: Ann Marie Damian
Design and Layout: Pamela J. Getchell

Library of Congress Cataloging-in-Publication Data

Geer, Beverley, 1951-
   Notes for serials cataloging / Beverley Geer and Beatrice L. Caraway ; foreword by Regina Romano Reynolds. -- 2nd ed.
    xvi, 168 p. 17x25 cm.
   Rev. ed. of: Notes for serials cataloging / Nancy G. Thomas. 1st ed. 1986.
   Includes bibliographical references and index.
   ISBN: 1-56308-449-X
   1. Cataloging of serial publications. 2. Notes (Cataloging)-- Specimens. 3. Anglo-American cataloguing rules. 4. Descriptive cataloging--Rules. I. Caraway, Beatrice L., 1953- . II. Thomas, Nancy G. Notes for serials cataloging. III. Title.
Z695.7.T46 1998
025.3'432--dc21   97-36865
                                                  CIP

CONTENTS

FOREWORD

Even though most catalogers will never write a book, their prose is nonetheless read daily throughout the world via the catalog records they create. Notes on catalog records are used by researchers, reference librarians, and other catalogers to help flesh out bare-bones bibliographic information originally designed to fit on a 3 X 5-inch card. In the past 25 years, the audience for notes on catalog records has expanded from the local library community, to national shared database users, and now to the global Internet community. As the number and variety of catalog users have increased, so has the need for notes to be cogent, clear, and useful. These same circumstances make this new edition of a classic tool for serial catalogers all the more welcome.

Notes play a crucial role in serial records. Because a serial's description is based on the earliest issue, notes provide the only means to convey current information that might be critical to the identification or use of the serial. Notes also allow the cataloger to describe important idiosyncrasies of a particular publication. And only serial catalogers know just how idiosyncratic some serials can be! Although my own experience is that publishers can come up with unique situations as fast as catalogers can devise notes for them, the examples of notes for almost every conceivable publishing quirk packed into this book will go a long way towards helping catalogers cope with these quirks.

In this second edition, Beverley Geer and Beatrice Caraway have ably restored the usefulness of a resource that some serial cataloging sections were tempted to chain to a table when it first appeared in 1986. In the intervening years, tags and tagging practices have changed, format integration has produced new types of notes for serials, and the new world of electronic resources has necessitated a new world of electronic resource notes. All of these changes are thoroughly represented in this new edition.

The Introduction to the first edition states that, "*Notes for Serial Cataloging* is a selective compilation of notes to be used as examples in constructing that ever-elusive 'perfect note.' " In today's world of "better, cheaper, faster" cataloging, I believe that clarity is a better goal than perfection, and efficiency a better approach than agonizing. And, it is precisely this book's ability to provide models and inspirations for more quickly and easily constructing useful and informative notes that makes it such a valuable resource for today's time-pressed cataloger.

Serial catalogers well know that cataloging is both an art and a science. As someone who has always felt that the creation of notes typifies the artful side of cataloging, I want to thank Geer and Caraway for inviting me to participate in the revitalization of a work that contributes to both the art of cataloging and the science of efficient record creation.

Regina Romano Reynolds
May 1, 1997

ACKNOWLEDGMENTS

We are indebted to a great number of people. We must thank Marilyn Kercher, our friend and colleague at the Columbus (Ohio) Metropolitan Library, who suggested that we take on this project. We have enjoyed the support and encouragement of everyone at Coates Library, Trinity University, most especially Richard W. Meyer, Director, and Ruby E. Miller, Assistant Director for Technical Services and Automation. We are grateful to Robert Blystone, Professor of Biology, and Steve Curry, Senior Programmer/Analyst, both of Trinity University, for guiding us along the path of high technology. We heartily thank our colleagues in the field who sent us examples of notes and helped us sort out the complexities, especially Steve Shadle, Serials Cataloger at the University of Washington, and Pamela Simpson, Serials Cataloger at Pennsylvania State University. Steve also spent many hours good-naturedly reviewing the manuscript and providing well-reasoned advice on the more complex aspects of linking entries. We are very grateful to the good people at OCLC and the Library of Congress who gave us permission to use and cite their impeccable documentation. We also acknowledge and thank Rosanna O'Neil and Nancy Thomas, the editors of the first edition, who provided us with the solid foundation on which this new edition rests. Without a doubt, we would have gotten nowhere without the support, assistance, and advice of Regina Romano Reynolds, Head of the National Serials Data Program at the Library of Congress.

README.PLZ

We are so pleased that you are reading this!! Although the title of the book describes what the book is, this section provides you with information on how the book was constructed so that you can use it with confidence and understanding.

Notes for Serials Cataloging, 2nd edition, is a selective compilation of notes to be used as examples in constructing notes in serial bibliographic records. The notes were taken from the OCLC online union catalog and from the *CONSER Editing Guide*, 1994 edition. As was done in the previous edition, we selected notes that could be described as generic: those which, with some adaptation, could be applied to serials. Many of the notes are basic, but we also selected notes that describe more complex situations.

For the most part, the language used in notes is free-form. We made no effort to prescribe wording but provided catalogers with examples upon which creation of notes can be based. In many cases, the choice of wording is subjective. However, there are rules of punctuation that should be followed, and, of course, the rules of grammar always apply. Except for making the most minor corrections, we transcribed the notes as we found them. When it seemed advisable to do so, we supplied a "better" variation on the note in square brackets at the end of the entry.

We generally have entered the notes as a finished product, i.e., with punctuation and print constants. It is important that you consult documentation relevant to your system to determine which marks of punctuation and which print constants are machine supplied.

ORGANIZATION

As in the previous edition, we have arranged the notes in MARC field order. We have provided definitions and scope notes from *OCLC Bibliographic Formats and Standards*, 2nd edition, and the *CONSER Editing Guide*, 1994 edition. Within some fields we have provided topical subdivisions to make it easier for catalogers to find the appropriate examples.

All notes are included. The implementation of format integration and the creation of new varieties of notes to describe electronic serials opened the door for the potential use of nearly fifty 5XX notes, plus the notes generated by the various second indicators in the 246 field. Obviously, not all notes are appropriate for serials. For example, it is unlikely that you will find a serial dissertation, and so the 502 Dissertation Note will not be used (never say never!). In the definition/scope area of each field, we have indicated which notes are generally not used in serials and have not provided examples of those notes. Obsolete notes that were described in the *OCLC Bibliographic Formats and Standards*, 2nd edition, are also included.

The section on the 580 Linking Entry Complexity Note is arranged by related linking entry field. Our premise is that if a cataloger determines which linking field (765-787) is necessary, he or she can then determine whether the linking entry is sufficient to explain the relationship or if a 580 note is needed to explain the relationship. Please bear in mind that these linking fields behave differently in different systems, so the decision to create a 580 note will depend on the system used. We have not given as examples those 580 notes that merely restate the simple information that would be supplied by the standard print constant and subfields of a linking entry field if the automated system were fully functional with regard to such fields. For example:

> Continued by: Acta crystallographica. Section A, Foundations of crystallography (See OCLC #1460869 or LCCN 86-643046 for the complete record.)

A fully functional 785 field would generate this note. If your system does not, you will need to construct a 580 note in addition to the 785 field.

Often it is helpful to read the note in the context of the record in which it appears. To that end, we have supplied a list of cataloging records from which the notes were taken. The list includes the author (when present in the record), title, the Library of Congress Control Number (when present in the record), and the OCLC record number. Please remember that because rules and conventions change, so will the records change and many of the examples we cite may change or disappear altogether.

Lastly, we have included a general index and list of suggested readings.

We hope that this tool will serve you well, whether you are a cataloger, an educator, or someone striving to understand this particularly important aspect of serials cataloging.

VARYING FORM OF TITLE

DEFINITION/SCOPE

OCLC Bibliographic Formats and Standards, 2nd ed.:
Varying forms of title associated with the item, whether or not the title is on the item. Use field 246 if a title differs substantially from the title statement in field 245 and if it contributes to further identification of the item.

CONSER Editing Guide, 1994 ed.:
Field 246 is used to record varying forms of the title appearing on different parts of the serial, portions of the title proper, or alternative forms of titles as prescribed by LCRI 21.30J.

Field 246 may be used for the following:
1) To provide online access by title.
2) To generate a title added entry for a variant form, when desired, on output.
3) To generate a note on output

The first indicator regulates the generation or output of a note and/or added entry. Cataloging rules and CONSER policy (Cf. AACR2 rule 21.30J and corresponding LCRI) will in most cases, determine whether or not an added entry should be made.

The second indicator specifies the type of title recorded in field 246. It is used to generate a display constant that generally precedes titles when notes are generated from this field, i.e., when the first indicator is set to a value other than 0 or 1.

◆ Editors' note: The *CONSER Editing Guide* in conjunction with documentation from your bibliographic utility and your local system will provide guidance on how to generate notes and title added entries using field 246. If your local system uses field 246 as it is defined, the following categories of notes can be generated (otherwise they are recorded in the 500 General Note). PLEASE

NOTE that the text of each note is presented in its final, punctuated form. Please consult the documentation referred to above for information on what punctuation is system supplied.

Notes generated by the cataloger:

Second indicator ƀ (no information provided): Use for variant titles for which a special display or note is needed or when you want a special note that is not accommodated by other second indicator values. In this kind of note the cataloger provides wording describing the source of the title in a ǂi and records the title to which access is being given in a ǂa.

1. Introductory issue called: Chicago daily herald.
2. Title on reference manual: U.S. government periodicals index on CD-ROM.
3. Title on home page: Human retroviruses and AIDS compendium on line.
4. Title on database selection menu: NewsBank NewsFile/CD NewsBank.
5. Title in copyright statement: APL online.
6. Title on Windows icon: CGSB electronic catalog.
7. Title on table of contents page: Notices of the AMS.
8. At head of title: InfoTax.
9. Title on documentation: Opal United States immigration law library. Forms.
10. Also known as: Electronic journal of extension.
11. Added Japanese title on documentation: Kishōchō kaiyō kansoku shiryō.
12. Installation guides have French title: Guide statistique de l'énergie.
13. Added homepage title: CPF online.
14. Home page title: Journal of artificial intelligence research.
15. Default title for Windows program group: TESS for Windows-CDRom.
16. List name: AIDSBKRV.
17. Listserve name: BMMR-L.
18. WWW issues for Oct. 15, 1995-   have added title: Botanical electronic news.
19. Has subtitle: Ancient theater today.

Notes generated using print constants:

Second indicator 2 (distinctive title): Distinctive titles are special titles appearing on individual issues of serials in addition to the regular title.

Distinctive titles (e.g., theme title of a conference) should not be confused with individual titles within a monographic series.

1. Distinctive title: Commodities in industry, 1940.
2. Distinctive title: Campus planning, 1967.

Second indicator 3 (other title): Other titles include variant forms of the title found on the piece in a location not covered by other second indicator values. Do not use this indicator for a variant form found on the chief source or for titles mentioned in a 5XX note. This value may be used for the following types of titles: half-titles, masthead titles, or colophon titles.

1. Other title: UAW ammunition.
2. Other title: Annals of sociology, <1962-73>

Second indicator 4 (cover title): A cover title is the title printed on the original covers of a publication or lettered or stamped on the publisher's binding (as distinguished from the title lettered on the cover by a bindery). This note is used only when the cover is not the chief source. Do not confuse with the "Title from cover" note which is used when the cover substitutes as the chief source.

1. Cover title: State publications monthly checklist, <July 1976>-1994.
2. Cover title: Qantas annual report.
3. Cover title: Statistics of criminal and other offenses, 1969-

Second indicator 5 (added title page title): This is usually a title in another language found on a title page preceding or following the title page used as the chief source or at the end of the publication, sometimes in an inverted format. If the added title page appears at the back of the publication and in addition, there is a variant form of the added title page title found on the back cover, this title may be given in field 246 with second indicator value 3.

1. Added title page title: Rapport annuel du ministre, Loi sur l'assurance-récolte.
2. Added title page title: Murshid al-Sudān, <1982-1983>

Second indicator 6 (caption title): A caption title is the title printed at the head of the first page of text.

1. Caption title: IEEE control systems magazine.
2. Caption title: Annual report on the working of the Reserve Bank of India and Trend and progress of banking in India.

Second indicator 7 (running title): A running title is the title printed on the top or bottom of pages of the publication.

1. Running title: B.E.E.C. bulletin.
2. Running title: JACCH, <1976->

Second indicator 8 (spine title): The title found on the spine of the publication. The title must be a publisher's title and not a binder's title.

1. Spine title: Acta biologica.
2. Spine title: Knoxville College alumni directory.

INTRODUCTION

DEFINITION/SCOPE

OCLC Bibliographic Formats and Standards, 2nd ed.:
Use field 500 for general notes. Use other 5XX fields for specialized notes. Use a separate 5XX field for each note. Use specialized notes if additional data or a distinctive word or phrase introducing the note provides access to the record.

CONSER Editing Guide, 1994 ed.:
Notes in serial records fall into two categories:
  1) Notes input in the 5XX note fields, and;
  2) Notes generated on output from other fields in the record (e.g., 246, 310, etc.).

The 5XX fields contain general notes (field 500) and specific notes (fields 525, 550, etc.) that cannot be generated from another field.

5XX notes are input in numeric tag order, with the exception of fields 533 and 539. Fields 533 and 539 are input following all other 5XX notes. If necessary, specific instructions are provided within individual fields for the multiple input of notes having the same tag number.

◆ Editors' note: See also the section above on using the 246 and its various indicators to produce general notes.

GENERAL NOTE

DEFINITION/SCOPE

OCLC Bibliographic Formats and Standards, 2nd ed.:
Field 500 contains unformatted notes that give bibliographic information not present elsewhere in the record, or information that is present elsewhere but that must be repeated in field 500 to generate an intelligible note. Use field 500 for any note for which no specific tag has been defined.

CONSER Editing Guide, 1994 ed.:
Field 500 is used for unformatted notes for whenever the other 5XX note fields are not applicable. Multiple 500 fields may be input in the order prescribed by AACR2R. The "Description based on" note, when used, is always input as the last 500 field.

INFORMAL SCOPE NOTES

A. General contents information
1. Lists names, addresses and work in progress of all members.
2. Looseleaf including: newsletter, evaluations, new releases and cumulative index.
3. Each issue for -1992 consists of a list of documents and an index, which are issued combined, 1993-
4. Some issues devoted to individual authors.
5. Each issue covers a different subject.
6. Each issue covers a particular geographic area or city.
7. The Oct. issue of each year is the annual report of the Association.
8. Fourth quarter issue contains also the annual report for the fiscal year.
9. Contains OCLC online union catalog bibliographic records.

10. Accompanied by: computer disks, manual, data card, header card display, and laser lens cleaning disk.
11. Contains county and city data files, current population survey files, county business pattern files, regional economic information system files, TIGER and decennial census files, intercensal population estimates files, and ZIP-city-county reference files.

B. "Includes" statements (For examples of separately published titles, see "580 Linking Entry Complexity Note.")
   1. Includes syllabus paragraphs of the opinions of the Attorney General of Ohio as they are released.
   2. Includes printed introduction and bibliographic key.
   3. Includes reproduction of t.p. and plates; text in Japanese translation, with notes in Japanese added.
   4. Vols. 1-6 include music; v. 7-17 consist exclusively of actual music without articles on musical subjects.
   5. Some numbers include reports submitted to its general meeting.
   6. Vols. 9-17 include decisions of the War Labor Board.
   7. Vol. for 1980 includes index for 1977-1979 of ALEC's suggested state legislation.
   8. One folded map included.
   9. Some issues include Appendixes; some Appendixes issued under separate cover.
   10. Includes also a microfilm ed. of: Business collection, and: Magazine collection.
   11. Discs include an optional multimedia program (with specific memory and hardware requirements) called: Idea source.
   12. Includes read-only version of Pro-Cite software.
   13. Includes software to display data.
   14. Contains Folio Infobase software.
   15. Issues for 1995- also contain HTML-formatted abstracts called "Previews."
   16. Issues for <Oct. 31, 1993-> include: Title 10, Energy; Title 29, Labor; Title 40, Protection of Environment; and: Title 49, Transportation.
   17. First disk includes every article in MacTutor, vol. 1-8, 1985-1992 (MacTutor continued by MacTECH magazine); and Inside Macintosh, vol. 1-6.
   18. Vols. for 1993- include one issue each year called also Technical & software bulletin, which is accompanied by 2 disks, one a PC version and one a Macintosh version.

19. Contains latest version of STARS (Socioeconomic Time-series Access and Retrieval System), Text STARS, and Javelin PLUS software.
20. Includes annually issued diskette entitled: Synthesis reviews database, <1996->

C. Proceedings information
   1. Consists of proceedings of symposia.
   2. Consists of proceedings of meetings on biomaterials.
   3. Proceedings of various symposia held 1978-
   4. Some proceedings cover both spring and fall meetings.
   5. Based on the proceedings of a series of workshops.
   6. Vol. 1 consists of papers presented at an American Chemical Society Symposium.
   7. Vols. 1- include 6th- proceedings of the annual conference.
   8. Vols. 1-2 constitute proceedings of: Symposium on the Fracture Mechanics of Ceramics; 3- proceedings of: International Symposium on the Fracture Mechanics of Ceramics.
   9. Consists of the proceedings of the 6th- meeting of the International Society of Hypertension and other international meetings.
   10. Includes the papers and proceedings of the annual conference of the Australian Mining and Petroleum Law Association.
   11. Includes programs and brief proceedings of 1st-32nd annual meetings, 1911-1946 (the Society was inactive 1918-1921). No meetings held, 1944-1945.
   12. Vols. for 1898-1941, 1948-1956 include the Society's proceedings (primarily abstracts of papers presented at the 10th-53rd annual meetings, and the 1948-1956 fall meetings).

D. General coverage information (For report year coverage information, see "515 Numbering Peculiarities Note.")
   1. Data based on previous year.
   2. Some issues include data from previous time periods.
   3. Vol. for 1980 is cumulative for 1978-1980.
   4. Includes revised data for varying numbers of years.
   5. Includes preliminary data and projections for the following two years.
   6. Work objectives and proposals for 12-month period beginning July 1, and accomplishments for prior 12 months.
   7. Issue for 1981/1982 includes bibliographies for reports published the preceding year.

8. Each issue covers films released the previous year as well as some films of the past.
9. Vols. for 1981- list publications catalogued by the University Library, 1981- irrespective of date and place of publication, and includes items published after 1975 not previously listed.
10. Each issue includes a bibliography of art books published in the United Kingdom during the preceding quarter; issue for Mar. 1982 covers books published June-Dec. 1981.
11. Vol. for 1980 covers the results of the research conducted in the last 5 years beginning 1976.
12. Includes a five year plan for the following five years and an accountability report for the previous year.
13. Each no. will index articles published during the semester preceding the issue of the Index.
14. Vol. for 1975 indexes publications of the U.S. Geological Survey, 1879-1974.
15. Each disk is cumulative.

E. General translation notes (For notes concerning language(s) of text, see "546 Language Note.")
    1. Cover-to-cover translation from Russian.
    2. Articles translated from Russian periodicals.
    3. Translations of articles from Chinese publications.
    4. Translation of articles from major Chinese physics and astronomy journals.
    5. Translation of papers from Soviet and Eastern European periodicals.
    6. First issue each year devoted to translations into English; the second, into all other languages (first series only).

NOTES ABOUT TITLES

A. Source of the title
    1. Title from title screen.
    2. Title from letter of transmittal.
    3. Title from table of contents page.
    4. Title from the case supplied by the publisher of reprint edition.
    5. Title from disc label.
    6. Title appears only on the colophon of many issues.
    7. Title from readme file.
    8. Title from home page.
    9. Title from table of contents caption of ftp version.

B. Title proper information
   1. Each title includes the name of a municipality (e.g., Analisis geoeconomico Atoyac, Analisis geoeconomico Atotonilco El Alto, etc.).
   2. Vols. for 1982- carry in the title the year of issue, i.e., Compensation 82.
   3. Each issue carries also in its title the number of articles, e.g., Seks faglige bidrag.
   4. Section designation at foot of cover constitutes part of title. Cf. Publisher's letter.
   5. Vols. for <1919-> have title only in characters.
   6. Some issues lack title.
   7. Vol. for 1978 issued without title.
   8. First issue was untitled when first published and was reprinted in Dec. 1969.
   9. Vol. 56, no. 5 has an additional cover bearing its former title.
   10. Lacks title screen.
   11. Title on title screen varies according to operating system used: PC-TESS; or: Mac-TESS.
   12. Issues for <-Q.4/92> lack title screen.

C. Miscellaneous title information
   1. Some issues lack the other title information.
   2. Some numbers have sub-title: Midwest edition.
      ✦ [AACR2R: subtitle]
   3. Subtitle varies; some numbers issued without subtitle.
   4. Subtitle varies to reflect the titles incorporated.
   5. Subtitle fluctuates between Ergänzungsband and Supplement depending upon the language of the issue.
   6. Each issue has also a distinctive title.
   7. Some issues also have a theme title.

D. Language of title/parallel title information (For notes concerning language(s) of text, see "546 Language Note.")
   1. Title also appears in other languages.
   2. Order of titles varies.
   3. Title order varies frequently.
   4. Order of titles alternates.
   5. Order of series titles varies.
   6. Order of titles on title page rotates each year.
   7. Order of titles varies with language of text.

8. Titles also in the other official languages of the Communities.
9. Finnish title precedes the Latin one in v. 1-25.
10. Reports for 1974-1975, 1976-1977, and 1977-1978 have title in English preceding title in Afrikaans.
11. Vols. for Jan./June 1953-v. 5, no. 15 have parallel title: Philatelist.
    ✦ [This note could also be input as 246. The *CONSER Cataloging Manual* Module 6.4.1 recommends the following wording: Vols. for Jan./June 1953-v. 5, no. 15 have title in English: Philatelist.]
12. Some bilingual English and French numbers issued with parallel title: Rapport technique/Programme "bonite."
    ✦ [This note could also be input as 246. The *CONSER Cataloging Manual* Module 6.4.1 recommends the following wording: Some bilingual English and French numbers issued with title also in French: Rapport technique/Programme "bonite."]
13. Parallel title varies: Income and product, Puerto Rico, <1977-1978, 1981>
    ✦ [This note could also be input as 246. The *CONSER Cataloging Manual* Module 6.4.1 recommends the following wording: English language title varies: Income and product, Puerto Rico, <1977-1978, 1981>]
14. Parallel title dropped with issue for Jan. 1971.
    ✦ [*CONSER Cataloging Manual* Module 6.4.1 recommends the following wording: Title in [language] dropped with issue for Jan. 1971.]
15. No. 6- dropped parallel titles.
    ✦ [*CONSER Cataloging Manual* Module 6.4.1 recommends the following wording: No. 6- dropped titles in [languages]]
16. English title only, 1964-1968; 1980-
17. Main menu displays the following titles: IMI bibliography; IMB on CD-ROM; IMB auf CD-ROM; IMB sur CD-ROM.

E. Names of titles within a serial (not issued separately) (For names of titles within a serial issued separately, see "580 Linking Entry Complexity Note.")
   1. Includes section entitled: Tax laws enacted.
   2. Includes section "Geographischer Literaturbericht" (title varies) which was issued as a separately paged suppl. to v. 32-55, 1886-1909.
   3. Every third year, 1980-19 includes section: Prevention profile; issues for 1992- some v. include section: Healthy people 2000 review.

4. Contains two sections: Coin news, and: Medal news, which have separate caption titles and pagings, 1981-
5. Issues for <1989-> include insert: Index to selected stars.
6. Includes booklet: Preface and list of contributing libraries ([8 p.] ; 11 x 15 cm.).
7. One issue each year consists of a buyers' guide called "Green Book."
8. Vols. for <1976-> consist of: Alphabetical directory, Geographical directory, Areas of interest code, with those for 1979-1980 containing also: By-laws.
9. Includes separately titled sections: The virtual square; and: the cyberspace monitor.

F. Varying forms of title
   1. Title varies slightly.
   2. Title alternates irregularly: Relatório.
   3. In the editorial for v. 1, no. 1 called: Journal of oil and petroleum pollution.
   4. Winter number also has title: Studies by members of SCMLA.
   5. Vol. 6 has title: Current trends in life science.
   6. Some no. have title: Racial ethnic brotherhood.
   7. Some issues are cumulations with title: Anuario bibliográfico ecuatoriano.
   8. One issue each volume, v. 6- called also: Ninth Circuit survey; one issue each volume, v. 8- called also: Women's law forum.
   9. Beginning in 1980 some issues have title: Knitting times newsweekly. One issue each month, Mar. 24-Dec. 1980 has title: Apparel world.
   10. Vols. for even-numbered years have title: National accounts.
   11. Title in colophon of dai 2-gō, published in 1982 in romanization: Haiku Bungakkan kiyo.
   12. Vol. 22, no. 2 called Legislative research checklist due to printing error.

G. Alternate issues (For notes concerning numbering shared with other titles, see "515 Numbering Peculiarities Note.")
   1. Alternate issues titled: Geology and geography; Geophysics and geodesy.
   2. Composed of alternately issued vols. with subtitles: Fundamentals; Applications; Equipment; and; Systems.

3. Vols. for 1973- include: International monographs on early child care, as alternate issues of the journal.
4. Beginning in 19 - monthly issues issued alternately as Brewers edition and Wholesaler edition; weekly issues issued as tabloid with edition statement varying.

IMPRINT VARIATION INFORMATION

(For publication information in regard to issuing bodies, see "550 Issuing Body Note.")

1. Distributor information taken from label.
2. Imprint varies: Vol. 3- published in Beaumont, Tex. ; <v. 19- > in Lincoln, Neb.
3. Imprint varies: New York : Columbia University Press, c1983-
4. Place of publication varies.
5. Published: Budapest : Lehrbuchverlag, 1979-
6. Nos. 1-5 published in New York; New ser., Vol. 1, no. 1-v. 4, no. 2 published in Boston, Mass.
7. Vols. for 1975/76- published: London : Studio Vista ; New York : Van Nostrand Reinhold.
8. Issued at: Salem State College, Salem, MA, Oct. 1981-
9. Also distributed by Westlaw, Lexis, and on an experimental basis, by Internet.

ISSUING INFORMATION

A. Physical description
   1. Reproduced from typed catalog cards.
   2. Some no. reproduced from typescript; some no. loose-leaf.
   3. In looseleaf folders.
   4. Loose-leaf for monthly updating.
   5. Loose-leaf for updating between editions.
   6. Beginning with v. 2, current issues in loose-leaf format; each vol. issued also in bound form after completion.
   7. Issued as advance sheets replaced periodically by bound vols.
   8. Published in journal-sized folders containing microfiches (10.5 x 15 cm.).
   9. Vols. for Sept. 1980- issued in newspaper format.
   10. Vols. for 1978- issued also in softcover edition with the cover title: Access: law.

    11. Introduction available only in printed form.
    12. Originally published in print beginning in 1989; issued online in addition to print beginning in 1995.

B. Updates and revisions (For updates that are supplements, see "525 Supplement Note"; for named updates, see "580 Linking Entry Complexity Note.")
    1. Kept up-to-date with annual replacement pages.
    2. Kept up-to-date between editions with revision pages.
    3. Each edition is kept up-to-date by quarterly cumulated releases.
    4. Updates the base volume published in 1971.
    5. Updated monthly, may be updated by German/French/Dutch edition also.
    6. Five year updates are planned.
    7. Each issue updates preceding issue.
    8. Each list is an addendum to the previous list.
    9. Vol. 1, Federal laws, replaces the opinions published in the loose-leaf binder v. 5, Decisions, from v. 1, 1970-

C. Miscellaneous issuing information
    1. Limited edition of 350 copies.
    2. Issued each year in preliminary and in final form.
    3. Abstracts also issued biweekly in computer printout form, Jan. 1983-
    4. The preface in no. 4 (1979) indicates that no. 1-3 were published under an earlier title.
    5. No. 1 is a reprint of the original issue which was privately printed; it contains the archaeological papers only, the preliminary matter (p. 1-54) being omitted.
    6. Some issues consist, wholly or in part, of preprints.
    7. Issued also in an annual summary.
    8. Includes separate classified section, published fortnightly.
    9. Each vol. published in separate pts. called "svituk," each devoted to a particular subject, e.g., Zheleznitsi, number of pts. varies.
    10. Beginning with fall 1982, for sale by the Supt. of Docs.
    11. Some issues not for sale by Supt. of Docs.
    12. G.P.O. sales statement incorrect in document.
    13. Many subseries issued within this publication.
    14. Issued also in Plant ed.; some articles included in both eds.

MISCELLANEOUS GENERAL NOTES

1. At head of title, no 9- : Centre national de la recherche scientifique, Centre régional de publications de Meudon-Bellevue.
2. Individual issues of copy from which fiche was made lack title pages.
3. Contents alternate monthly: Original articles in odd numbered months; Current literature in even-numbered months.
4. Part of the illustrative matter is folded.
5. Part of the illustrative material in pocket.
6. Map on folded leaf in pocket.
7. Some issues have different cochairmen.
8. Vols. for 1980, <1983>-198 printed for the use of the Committees on Foreign Affairs and on Science and Technology; 1981 for the use of the Committee on Foreign Affairs; <1987>-199 for the use of the Committee on Science, Space, and Technology and the Committee on Foreign Affairs; 199 -1995 for the use of the Committee on Science and the Committee on International Relations.
9. Vols. for 19 have section and separate t.p. in Arabic.
10. Each edition has Ernst & Whinney stock number.
11. Issues prior to Jan. 1978 were classed: A 89.8:(v.nos.&nos.); issues for Jan. 1978-Sept. 1980 were classed: A 105.19:(v.nos.nos.).
12. Issued with United Nations publications sales no.
13. Yearbooks for 1948- issued with the United Nations publications sales no.: 1949.X111.1.
14. Supt. of Docs. class for the annual summary is: C 3.158:MA-22Q.
15. Sometimes referred to as: Blue-covered section.
16. Not to be confused with an earlier publication of the same name, issued in Santiago de Chile.
17. Not to be confused with an earlier title of the same name published 1976 by F.A. Davis.
18. This series of Proceedings is independent of the earlier one of the same title, published in 3 parts, 1877-1895.
19. Published as: Bicentennial edition, 1975.
20. Vols. for 1968-1970 also issued as departmental ed. by the Dept. of Health, Education, and Welfare; <1983>-1988 also issued as departmental ed. by the U.S. Environmental Protection Agency.

DESCRIPTION BASED ON NOTES

1. Description based on: [1980].
2. Description based on printout of online display; title from caption.
3. Description based on printout of online display of: No. 4; title from caption.
4. Description based on: Aug. 1994; title from disc label.
5. Description based on: V5.11 (April 1996 release); title from welcome screen.
6. Description based on: Vol. 244, no. 2 (Nov. 1994); title from gopher version table of contents.
7. Description based on: Release 3.0 (1996); title from search screen header.
8. Description based on: Quarter 1-4/92 (Jan. 1992 to Dec. 1992); title from about database display.
9. Description based on demonstration issue: 6404, published 1994; title from journal home page.

EDITORS

1. Editor: 4th-5th ed., F. G. Ruffner; 6th-11th ed., M. Fisk.
2. Editor: Cuda Lee Brown.
3. Editors: Kenneth Sherwood and Loss Pequeño Glazier.
4. Edited 1964-69 by K.I. Porter.

"WITH" NOTE

DEFINITION/SCOPE

OCLC Bibliographic Formats and Standards, 2nd ed.:
Notes about separate works (usually with distinctive titles) contained in a physical item that are published, released, issued, or executed together **without** a collective title. Precede the data in the field with the word "With:" or "Issued with:", etc. However, catalog items lacking a collection title with no one work predominating as a unit.

If the note is a local "with" note, use field 590.

Because this note is not generally used in serial records, it is not defined in *CONSER Editing Guide*, 1994 ed. See "580 Linking Complexity Note."

DISSERTATION NOTE

DEFINITION/SCOPE

OCLC Bibliographic Formats and Standards, 2nd ed.:
Brief, formal notes that indicate that the item is an academic dissertation presented in partial fulfillment of the requirements for a degree. Use field 502 to explicitly state that the item is a thesis.

If the note is **relating** an item to a thesis (e.g., Based on, First published as, Also published as a thesis), use field 500.

Because this note is not generally used in serial records, it is not defined in *CONSER Editing Guide*, 1994 ed.

BIBLIOGRAPHIC HISTORY NOTE (OBSOLETE)

DEFINITION/SCOPE

"This field for books, music, and computer files was made obsolete because according to the guidelines agreed upon for separate notes its continued existence could not be justified; the information can be recorded in field 500 (General Note)"—*Format Integration and Its Effect on the USMARC Bibliographic Format*, 1995 ed.

BIBLIOGRAPHY, ETC. NOTE

DEFINITION/SCOPE

OCLC Bibliographic Formats and Standards, 2nd ed.:
Notes about a bibliography, discography, filmography, and/or other bibliographic references in an item. It may also note the presence of a bibliography, etc. in accompanying material that is described in the record. For multipart items, including serials, the note may pertain to all parts or to a single part of issue.

Use field 504 when the presence of an index is also mentioned in a bibliography note.

CONSER Editing Guide, 1994 ed.:
Field 504 contains information concerning the presence of important bibliographies or discographies in the serial. The bibliography/ discography note may pertain to all issues or a single issue of the serial.

1. "Bibliography of Texas legends": no. 3, p. [255]-260.
2. Includes section "Bibliographie", 1924-49.
   ✦ [AACR2R: 1924-1949]

FORMATTED CONTENTS NOTE

(See also 515, Issuing Peculiarities)

DEFINITION/SCOPE

OCLC Bibliographic Formats and Standards, 2nd ed.:
Contents notes contain the titles of separate works or parts of an item. They may also include statements of responsibility associated with the works or parts. Volume numbers and other sequential designations are included in the note, but chapter numbers are omitted.

Use field 505 for **formal** (formatted) contents notes. If the note is **informal** (unformatted), use field 500.

Because this note is not generally used in serial records, it is not defined in *CONSER Editing Guide,* 1994 ed.

RESTRICTIONS ON ACCESS NOTE

DEFINITION/SCOPE

OCLC Bibliographic Formats and Standards, 2nd ed.:
Note about limitations or restrictions on the use of an item or collection. Use to describe restrictions that pertain to all copies or issues.

If a note merely indicates the intended audience of a publication and does not imply restricted access, use field 521.

If the note indicates terms governing use of materials after access has been granted, use field 540.

Use field 355 when the security information is too specific to be handled in field 506.

CONSER Editing Guide, 1994 ed.:
Field 506 contains information about restrictions imposed on access to the serial. For published works, this field is used to record information on limited distribution.

1. Access restricted to registered users connecting from an approved IP address.
2. Access limited to individual subscribers and institutions with site license agreements.

SCALE NOTE FOR GRAPHIC MATERIAL

DEFINITION/SCOPE

OCLC Bibliographic Formats and Standards, 2nd ed.:
Notes about the scale of an architectural drawing or three-dimensional artifact.

For maps. Use field 507 for notes about scale of a map in pre-AACR2 records. Enter field 507 as the first note after field 300 or 4XX. If you are inputting current cataloging, use field 255 for statements of scale.

Because this note is not generally used in serial records, it is not defined in *CONSER Editing Guide*, 1994 ed.

508

CREATION/PRODUCTION CREDITS NOTE

DEFINITION/SCOPE

OCLC Bibliographic Formats and Standards, 2nd ed.:
Notes about credits for individuals or organizations (other than members of a cast) who have participated in the artistic or technical production of an item and have made contributions of special significance.

Use added entry fields (e.g., field 700) to enter formalized added entries for each name in field 508.

CONSER Editing Guide, 1994 ed.:
Field 508 is used for notes containing the names of persons or organizations, other than members of the cast, who have participated in the creation and/or production of the work. For serials, field 508 is used primarily for videorecordings.

For serials, designations (usually dates) may be given to show the span of issues for which the person or organization was associated with the production.

---

1. Producers: Jeff Lifton, 1986-
2. Co-produced by: American Library Association, and: Library Video Network.

CITATION/REFERENCES NOTE

DEFINITION/SCOPE

OCLC Bibliographic Formats and Standards, 2nd ed.:
Note about citations or references to published bibliographic de-scriptions or reviews of an item. Use to specify where an item has been cited or reviewed. Enter citations or references in a brief form (i.e., using generally recognizable abbreviations, etc.). Enter the actual text of a published description in field 520.

For serials, use to specify publications in which a serial has been indexed and/or abstracted and the dates of coverage, if known. The indexing and abstracting services referenced are primarily those issued for serials. However, certain monographic titles, particularly those that are standard reference tools in a subject area or that cover periods of an item **not** included in continuing publications, may be entered.

Note that field 510 is used when the indexing and/or review is external to the item represented by the bibliographic record. Field 555 (Cumulative Index/Finding Aids Note) is used when an index is an integral part of the item.

When the title of the source of the index, abstract, review, etc. changes, a separate field 510 is used for each title. When coverage changes, thus requiring a different value in the first indicator, a new field 510 with appropriate dates is added to the record.

CONSER Editing Guide, 1994 ed.:
Field 510 specifies where a serial has been indexed and/or abstracted and, if known, the dates of coverage or location within the source. Each abstracting/indexing service is tagged as a separate field. For rare serials, field 510 contains a bibliographic reference note.

This field is used when the indexing is external to the publication in hand. Field 555 is used when the index is an integral part of the publication and covers more than one volume or issue.

◆ Editors' note: The notes in this section are listed as they would appear on the catalog card, including print constants which can be applied to the note. For instructions on tagging the 510 field, see the *OCLC Bibliographic Formats and Standards*, the *CONSER Editing Guide*, or your bibliographic utility's documentation.

1. Indexed in its entirety by: Current index to journals in education.
2. Indexed selectively by: Computer & control abstracts.
3. Indexed by: Engineering index monthly.

PARTICIPANT OR PERFORMER NOTE

DEFINITION/SCOPE

OCLC Bibliographic Formats and Standards, 2nd ed.:
Note about the participants, players, narrators, presenter, or performers. In general, an on-screen narrator is recorded in field 511 and a voice-over narrator in field 508 (Creation/Production Credits Note).

CONSER Editing Guide, 1994 ed.:
For serials, field 511 is primarily used for sound recordings and videorecordings.

1. Commentators: Gregory P. Johnstone, Stephen W. Ireland, Clay M. Powell, J. David Watt.
2. Narrators: Nora Rawlinson, 1986-

EARLIER OR LATER VOLUMES SEPARATELY CATALOGED NOTE (OBSOLETE)

DEFINITION/SCOPE

"This field was made obsolete because it was considered to be LC-centric. The information can be recorded in field 500 (General Note) with a subfield ÷5 present containing the National Union Catalog symbol of the library to which the information pertains"—*Format Integration and Its Effect on the USMARC Bibliographic Format,* 1995 ed.

TYPE OF REPORT AND PERIOD COVERED NOTE

---

1. Quarterly technical progress report
2. Annual report

DATA QUALITY NOTE

DEFINITION/SCOPE

OCLC Bibliographic Formats and Standards, 2nd ed.:
Note about the general assessment of the quality of the data set constituting the item.

Because this note is not generally used in serial records, it is not defined in *CONSER Editing Guide*, 1994 ed.

NUMBERING PECULIARITIES NOTE

DEFINITION/SCOPE

OCLC Bibliographic Formats and Standards, 2nd ed.:
Unformatted notes giving irregularities and peculiarities in numbering or publishing patterns. Use also to show that a publication is issued in parts or revised editions, or to express report year coverage. Use for the following types of irregularities and peculiarities in numbering:

- double numbering
- combined issues or volumes
- confusion in use of series numbering or whole numbering systems
- publication of preliminary issues **not** included in the regular numbering
- numbering that does **not** begin with v. 1
- serials issued in parts, sections, or volumes
- unpublished items
- suspended publications

CONSER Editing Guide, 1994 ed.:
Field 515 contains an unformatted note giving irregularities and peculiarities in numbering or publishing patterns. It may also be used to show that a publication is issued in parts or revised editions, or to express report year coverage.

REPORT YEAR COVERAGE

(For general coverage information, see "500 General Note.")

1. Each report covers 5 years.
2. Reports cover 4th quarter data.
3. Report year ends Mar. 31 of the following year.
4. Periods covered by reports correspond to the academic years.
5. Vols. for 1977- cover calendar year and first half of following year.
6. Reports for Apr. 1979/Mar. 1980- cover Japanese fiscal years 1979-
7. Report covers financial year ending Dec. 31 of the preceding year.
8. Report covers first half of fiscal year; the Treasurer's annual report covers second half of fiscal year.
9. Each report covers 2 years and is published at the end of marketing season for the various states.
10. Report year irregular; first report covers Jan. 1938-Sept. 1939.
11. Report years for equalized assessed valuations and tax rates vary.
12. Each report contains cumulated monthly summaries covering an eight year period, i.e., 1967-1975.
13. Reports for -1985/1986 include projected statistics for -1986/1987.
14. Report cumulative for four quarters of the State fiscal year, <1980->; for the first two quarters of State fiscal year, <1982->
15. First report year covers period Apr. 5, 1978-Dec. 31, 1978.
16. Vol. for 1979 covers Apr. 1 through Dec. 31. Succeeding issues cover calendar year.
17. Report for 1979 covers 3 years, i.e., 1979-1981.
18. First report covers a three-year period; subsequent annual reports cover five-year periods.
19. Period covered by report for 1970/72 ends July 30; report year for 1972/73- ends Apr. 30.
20. The General periodicals index covers data for the last four years; the General periodicals index backfile covers data for the preceding four years; the Government publications index covers public documents issued by the legislative branches of the U.S. government beginning in 1976; the National newspaper index covers the last four years of the New York times (Late and National ed.), the Wall Street journal (Eastern and Western

ed.), the Christian science monitor (Western ed.), the Los Angeles times (Home ed.), and: the Washington post (Final ed.).
21. Current disc is cumulative and covers the most recent four years.
22. Specific dates of coverage are given in running display.
23. Backfiles for 1970-1991 issued on three discs: Jan. 1972-Dec.1978; Jan. 1979-Dec. 1984; 1984-Dec. 1991.

DOUBLE NUMBERING

1. Vols. also bear numbering in Dutch.
2. Two systems of numeric designation start with issue 7.
3. Issues also carry whole numbering.
4. Also numbered within each presidency.
5. No. 1-2 called 1. année; no. 1 called also v. 1, fasc. 1.
6. Issues for 1980/81-1981/82 called also Part II.
7. Vols. for Mar./June 1965- , called also New series.
8. Nr. 13- called also anul 11-
9. Vols. for winter 1979- called also issue #5-
10. Vols. for 1982- called also anno 1- = ser. 1-
11. Vols. for 1978- called also 6th annual report-
12. Vols. for 1980-1989 called also v. 15-24 in continuation of the numbering of: Oecologia plantarum.
13. Vol. 1, no. 1- called also v. 13, no. 1- continuing the numbering designation of the previous title.
14. Issues have both their own volume numbering and some volume numbering from Chemical geology (i.e., vol. 1 of Isotope geoscience also called v. 41 of Chemical geology; v. 2 of Isotope geoscience also called v. 46 of Chemical geology; v. 3 of Isotope geoscience also called v. 52 of Chemical geology; v. 15 of Isotope geoscience also called v. 101 of Chemical geology).
15. No. 1-3 called also v. 3, no. 1-2 and v. 4, no. 3 in continuation of ser. IV of the council's studies which this succeeds.
16. Has also whole numbers (odd numbers 589- assigned to Faraday transactions I; even numbers assigned to Faraday transactions II).
17. Issued irregularly in parts which, in v. 1-54 are numbered consecutively no. 1-220; in later vols. the consecutive numbering was discontinued.
18. Each issue carries also numbering derived from the initials of its author, e.g., NNM-1-'82.

19. Reports also numbered serially within list of all the Commission's reports.
20. Some no. are also numbered as suppl. to the parent journal: Allergy.
21. Some issues carry also the date of the Jewish calendar.
22. Both Christian and Hegira dates appear on pieces, but vol. designation follows Hegira dates.
23. Container spine also carries number: <961->
24. Designation includes coding for year in the first character, i.e., A = 1992, B = 1993, etc.; issue is indicated by "release" letter, i.e., Z = 1st release, Y = 2nd release, etc.

COMBINED ISSUES OR VOLUMES

1. Some issues combined.
2. Some numbers issued together.
3. Some numbers issued in combined form.
4. Some issues published in combined form.
5. Two sections issued together once a month.
6. Vol. 5, no. 1-4 issued combined.
7. Report for 1974/76 published in combined form in 1976.
8. Vols. for spring & summer 1979 and spring & summer 1982, issued in combined form.
9. Vol. 1, no.1-4 (summer 1982-spring 1983) published together in one volume.
10. Issued in combined volumes for 1937-1942 and for 1942-1944; issued annually thereafter.
11. Vol. 4, no. 1 has stamp which reads: "The special double issue contains vol. 4, nos. 1 & 2."
12. Each issue bears a combined numbering (e.g., no. 1-2).
13. Some no. published as combined issues with: Ethnic racial review.

NUMBERING INCONSISTENCIES OR IRREGULARITIES

A. Numbering lacking
1. Some issues lack numbering.
2. First issue lacks numeric designation.
3. Issue for May 1981 has no vol. number.
4. Vol. 1, no. 1-4 lack vol. and no. designations.

5. Issue for Oct. 1974 lacks numbering, but constitutes no. 169; May 1978-Mar. 1982 lack numbering; Apr. 1982-June 1982 also called v. 22, no. 7-v. 22, no. 9.
6. First issue is not numbered or dated but constitutes v. 1, no. 1.
7. Issues for Sept. 1979-mayo 1980 unnumbered but constitute año 1, no. 1-9.
8. Issues. for Nov. 1978-   carry no vol. number.
9. Issues for Sept. 1980-   lack vol. numbering but constitute v. 1, no. 1-
10. Vols. for   -1980 lack numeric and chronological designation.
11. First issue lacks numeric designation for the section title.
12. No. 1-4 lack title and numbering.
13. Earlier vols. are unnumbered and lack series title.
14. Some vols. lack series numbering.
15. Vols. 4-7 lack numbering of the main series.
16. Some issues have no vol. numbering but are called "Special issue."
17. Special issues may be unnumbered.
18. The first three vols. identified by date only; the last two by no. only.
19. Issues have no vol. or no. designations. Two issues may also carry the same month and year and not be duplicates.

B. Numbering dropped
    1. Vol. numbering ceased with v. 21, 1975.
    2. Numbering ceased with 3rd report, 1978-1979.
    3. New series designation dropped with v. 7, 1980.
    4. Vol. numbering ends with summer/fall 1978 issue; whole numbering begins with May 1979 issue.
    5. Issues identified by vol. and no. and date through v. 4, no. 9/10, 1981; by vol. and date, v. 5, fall 1981; by date only, winter 1982-Dec. 1987.
    6. The monthly issues were numbered consecutively (without vol. no.) from the beginning of the series to no. 155, Feb. 1931; with the no. for Mar. 1931, the consecutive numbering was discontinued and a numbering by vols. was adopted, the vol. for 1931 being v. 16 as reckoned from the first year of issue.
    7. Discs numbered with year and ed. (e.g., 1993-1).
    8. After vol. 19, no. 4, volume/number enumeration was dropped in favor of whole number enumeration. The next issue was no. 77.

C. Numbering added
    1. Vol. numbering begins with Aug. 1978 issue.
    2. Numbering began with v. 10, no. 4, May 1979.
    3. Numbering includes vol. designation with first issue for 1978.
    4. Issues 1 and 2 called Serial 1 and 2. Vol. designation assumed with v. 3, June 1975.
    5. Vol. numbering resumed with v. 20, no. 1 (Jan. 1980).
    6. Issue numbers supplied beginning with v. 45.

D. Numbering errors
    1. 37th omitted in numbering.
    2. Vol. 7, no. 7 repeated in vol. numbering.
    3. Vol. numbering irregular: occasional numbers repeated.
    4. Vol. numbering irregular: v. 28 repeated.
    5. Numbering for v. 1, no. 1 is repeated on issues for summer 1972 and for 1974.
    6. Weekly issue, Oct. 20, 1958 and monthly issue, Nov. 1958 both called v. 58, no. 11.
    7. Issues for Apr. 1970 and Sept. 1970 are both designated as instructional aid no. 45.
    8. Two reports numbered 45th: one covering the period from July 1-Dec. 31, 1925; the other for the calendar year 1926. Subsequent reports continue this numbering.
    9. Many issues misnumbered, v. 26, no. 10 repeated.
    10. Numbering very irregular.
    11. Frequent irregularities in numbering.
    12. Some irregularities in numbering; some numbers in v. 29 incorrectly numbered v. 30.
    13. Issue for 1978-79 incorrectly called 1977-78 on t.p.
    14. Issue for 1967 called 10-11, but constitutes 10 only.
    15. Vol. for 1979 constitutes 17th, but incorrectly marked 16th.
    16. Final issue called 1980 but constitutes final 1979 issue.
    17. Aug. 1977- issues called v. 100, no. 1- but constitute v. 99, no. 15- ; issues for Jan. 1978- repeat v. 100, no. 1- , corresponding to the numbering of NARD journal.
    18. Errors in numbering: v. 31, no. 2-3, Feb.-Mar. 1981 called v. 30, no. 2-3; v. 31, no. 5, May 1981 called v. 31, no. 4.
    19. Vol. 51, no. 610 incorrectly numbered v. 52, no. 610; correct numbering resumes with v. 51, no. 611.
    20. Vol. 2, no. 12 misnumbered as v. 2, no. 11; v. 2, no. 20-24 misnumbered as v. 2, no. 21-25.

21. Issue for Dec. 14, 1981 erroneously numbered v. 4, no. 37, following the numbering sequence of: NAHB builder.
22. Reprint edition covering Aug. 1938-Sept. 1939 numbered 1-299; erroneously printed as no. 1-229; no. 1 corresponds to no. 395 in the original numbering.
23. Numbering irregular: issue for spring/summer 1978 called also no. 3; issue for winter 1981 called also v. 5, no. 2.
24. The 44th regular session of the General Assembly was designated as the 45th regular session. The error in numbering has been continued by all the following assemblies.

E. Numbering shared with other titles (For general notes concerning alternate issues, see "500 General Note.")
    1. Vols. for 1958-1964, internumbered with: Issues.
    2. Issue numbering alternates with other Mitchell Manuals publications.
    3. Alternates vol. numbering with the Transactions of the Society of Mining Engineers of AIME and the Transactions of the Metallurgical Society of AIME.
    4. Numbering integrated with that of Ferroelectrics, Apr. 1982- . New series has separate numbering: Vol. 1, no. 1 (Aug. 1983)-
    5. Vol. 21 (1983) shares numbering with: American studies international newsletter.
    6. Issues are internumbered among these sections: supplement nos. 210-249 Section A, Pathology or Section B, Microbiology and immunology; no. 250- Section A, Pathology; Section B, Microbiology; or Section C, Immunology.
    7. Vol. numbering is part of a sequence which includes all sections of the journal with the common title: Mutation research.
    8. Follows the vol. and issue numbering of the print version.

F. Numbering that does not begin with vol. 1
    1. First issue is no. 2, 1980.
    2. Vol. 4 begins with no. 10 to conform to new publishers' publishing year.
    3. The vol. numbering is that of the original journal.
    4. Adopts its vol. numbering from other editions of: Today's education.
    5. Numbering and dates of issues pertain to: Le Praticien.

6. Vols. for 1961-1969 called "nouv. sér." in continuation of: Notulae systematicae; vols. for 1970-1981 called also: sér. 2.
7. Vol. 1, no. 1-4 called v. 104, no. 1-4 in continuation of the numbering of the Journal of experimental psychology.
8. Assumes the vol. numbering of: Annuaire international de l'éducation et de l'enseignement.
9. Assumes the vol. numbering of the parent periodical: Journal de physique.
10. Continues the numbering of Central-Zeitung für Optik und Mechanik.
11. Assumes the series and vol. numbering of: Bollettino della Unione matematica italiana.
12. Issue for Mar. 1953, constituting v. 1, no. 1, is numbered consecutively with American Association of Rehabilitation Therapists bulletin, as v. 3, no. 3.
13. Articles in issues for Jan. 1977- numbered consecutively boletín no. 228-
14. Each article is individually numbered following the numbering designation begun with Estudios CIEPLAN.

G. Inconsistencies in chronological designations
   1. Some issues lack dates.
   2. Vols. for <1980-> lack year designation.
   3. Issues for 1966 lack chronological designations; issues for 1967 misnumbered v. 1.
   4. Vol. 2, issue 4-v. 3 without date.
   5. Vol. 1, no. 1 without date but issued Mar. [?] 1978.
   6. Issues for Feb. 1980- omit name of month.
   7. Issues for Mar. 1971 and Aug. 1971 have only monthly designation.
   8. Cover and title page show different years.
   9. No. 1 has cover date: automne 1978.
   10. Title page of 1975 vol. erroneously designated 1976.
   11. No. 56/58 published in 1980 but constitutes last three issues for 1978.
   12. Chronological designation from spine.

H. Miscellaneous numbering inconsistencies or irregularities
   1. Numbering of some vols. incomplete due to irregular publication and combined issues.

2. Vols. for winter 1983-<spring 1990> have number on spine only; some issues combined.
3. Consists of even numbered issues only.
4. Numbering begins each year with 1.
5. Issues also numbered within the year.
6. Numbered 1-12 within each year, 1958-63; numbered 1-13, 1964-68?
   ◆ [AACR2R: 1958-1963 and 1964-1968]
7. Vols. for 1963-1965 numbered consecutively. Vols. for 1966-1978 start with no. 1 with each new year.
8. Issue numbering begins again following the publication of each ed. of: The Directory of directories.
9. Publication of a 2nd ser. began in 1971; 3rd ser. began in 1975; 4th ser. began in 1994.
10. The "new series" appearing on the cover of each number is in reference to earlier publications of the Association.
11. Vol. for Jan. 1976-Jan. 1978 called new ser., no. 1-22. With issue for Feb. 1978 cumulative numbering resumes with no. 221.
12. Vol. numbering changed in 1979 to coincide with New Guard.
13. Vol. numbering sequenced with the numbering of the Russian original.
14. Number of each issue includes initials of agency or other body for which the note was prepared, e.g., N-1000-AF.
15. Numbering includes the letter A, Jan. 1978- ; i.e., Vol. 83, no. A12.
16. Designated as pt. 1 whenever a corresponding supplement (called pt. 2) is issued.
17. Monthly issues for 1906 called v. 1; annual cumulation for 1906 called v. 2.
18. Pilot weekly edition issued Sept. 15, 1958 as vol. 1, no. 1. Beginning with Oct. 20, 1958-<Dec. 1964> issued as vol. 58, no. 11- , assuming numbering scheme of monthly issues. In Aug. 1966, weekly numbers issued as vol. 17, no. 6- while monthly issues continue former numbering scheme. Monthly issues adopt numbering scheme of weekly issues, beginning with vol. 21, no. 16 (Apr. 20, 1970)-
19. Mid-Sept. to mid-Oct. 1982 and mid-Oct. to mid-Nov. 1982, called opus 1, no. 1 and opus 1, no. 2 respectively.
20. Most vols. have no whole numbering; some vols. are numbered as parts of the whole series and/or as parts of the series of Eastern or Western conferences (e.g., Feb. 1956 called 9th Joint Conference and 4th Western Conference).

21. Issue no. for Dec. 1974-Dec. 1976 are continuous, i.e., v. 2 begins with no. 5.
22. Software version number included as part of title on container spine (e.g., Current facts 1).
23. Successive manuscripts are also identified with submission dates and are added to the article databases on a continuous basis.

ISSUING PECULIARITIES

A. General issuing peculiarities
  1. Not issued in numerical order.
  2. Vol. 17 comes between vols. 14 and 15.
  3. Numbers not issued in chronological order.
  4. Some numbers published out of chronological sequence.
  5. Issued irregularly between the regular biennial sessions.
  6. Vols. published consecutively, one each month, Oct. 1981-May 1982; autumn/winter 1982- issued concurrently.
  7. Last issue of each vol. is an annual index.
  8. Beginning in 1948 the last issue published in December of each year (except for 1958-1962 when it was the first issue in January) is called "Annual number."
  9. Jan. 1981-Jan. 1982 publisher experimented with publishing multiple issues some months targeted for specific professional interests, with the result that there were 3 issues, Physician, Nursing, Industrial hygiene, each month from Jan.-Apr. 1981, 2 issues, Safety and Health, for Sept. 1981 and Jan. 1982. The publisher has now abandoned this practice.
  10. Each annual issued supersedes all previous issues.
  11. Vol. 1- is reprint of no. 1-20-
  12. No. 4 and 5 not included in reprint ed.
  13. No. 1 (1978) is in a limited edition of 1000.
  14. Issue for Dec. 1978-Jan. 1979 was originally issued as a letter without serial title or numbering; copies were later titled and numbered retrospectively as no. 1.
  15. No. 1 not published in English.
  16. Vol. 2 published in 1979.
  17. Vol. 8, no. 33 issued 27th July 1979.
  18. Membership directory published every 3rd or 4th year in lieu of the annual research volume.

19. Vols. for 1969-<1973> called regular session; <1974-75->
    called fiscal year.
20. First report called Quarterly report (July-Sept. 1980); 2nd
    report called Six-month report (July-Dec.1980); 3rd report
    called Third quarterly report (1980-81).
21. Vols. for 1973-1979 suffixed "C"; 1980-1984 suffixed "C" (1st
    3 issues) and "D" (last 3 issues).
22. Beginning with v. 11, 1978 issues alternately called Part A:
    Chemical Analysis and Part B: Clinical and biochemical
    analysis; separate volume designation discontinued with v. 19,
    no. 1/2, 1986.
23. Issues for Sept. 1965-Aug. 1967 called alternately: Series A,
    Sciences; Series B, Managerial, or Series C, Bulletin; for Sept.
    1967-Aug. 1975 called, alternately: Theory or Application series.
24. In vols. for 1973-1983 odd numbered vols. cover Molecular
    aspects, even numbered vols. cover Cellular aspects. These vols.
    are published concurrently with one no. of each vol. issued
    each month, e.g., v. 131, no. 1 (Jan. 1973) covers Molecular
    aspects, and v. 132, no. 1 (Jan. 1973) covers Cellular aspects.
25. Published in two series: Scientific and Humanistic, which had
    alternating numbering.
26. Published also with variant vol. numbering and content "for
    official use only."
27. Articles in each vol. also published as separate no.
28. Vols. 1 and 2, indexing items published in 1980 and 1981,
    compiled retrospectively and issued as single cumulative issue
    for each year; beginning with v. 3, to be issued quarterly with
    the fourth issue being cumulative.
29. Discs for <1994-> also called: <940904->. Last two digits (04)
    identify Magazine index plus title.
30. Articles published prior to 1995 are not grouped into monthly
    issues.
31. Published one article at a time on the Internet.
32. Issues designated with "B" for backfile and "C" for current file.

B. Number of issues per volume, etc.
    1. Six issues per vol.; numbering within vols. begins in Jan. and
       July; issues for -1992 published in three vols.
    2. Each vol. consists of 4 numbers; 7 vols. per year, 1985-
    3. Each vol. contains three unnumbered issues.
    4. Four issues constitute a vol.

5. Vol. 1 complete in one issue.
6. Statistics for 1977-1979 issued as one vol.
7. Only three issues published for 1979.
8. Only one vol. issued to cover years 1968-1972.
9. Vol. 1, no. 1 was the only issue published for 1976.

C. Issued in named parts, sections, etc.
   1. Issued in 2 vols., the 2nd called Appendixes.
   2. Vol. for 1980 published in two issues, one called 1980 midyear.
   3. Issued in 2 vols., each with distinctive title: Vol. 1, Precolonial through reconstruction; Vol. 2, Reconstruction through the present.
   4. Issues for 1969-1974 published in 4 vols.; 1970/75-19   in 9 vols. covering various geographical regions; <1983-88-1984-89> in 5 vols., v. 1 being a summary and v. 2-5 covering various geographical regions.
   5. Vols. for 1952-1981- issued in two vols.: v. 1, Main aggregates; v. 2, Detailed tables. Vol. 2 does not cover same time period as v. 1 (e.g., v. 2 published in 1983 covers 1964-1981).
   6. Issued in multi-volume parts: M-1- : Media series; P-1- : Product series.
   7. Vols. for <1968-> issued in 2 vols.: v. 1: USSR and RSFSR; v. 2: Union Republics; vols. for <1973-> issued in 3 vols.: v. 1: National organizations; v. 2: RSFSR; v. 3: Union republics.
   8. Issued in 2 discs: Disc 1. Titles 1-26; disk 2. Titles 27-50.

D. Issued in unnamed parts, sections, etc.
   1. Issued in two vols. per year, 1981-1983; three vols. per year, 1984/1985.
   2. Issued in 2 v., 2nd ed.-
   3. Each edition consists of two individually released parts.
   4. Beginning with the 4th ed., each edition is published in several vols., each devoted to a specific academic area.
   5. Each v. issued in 16 pts., each with also a distinctive title.
   6. 1981 annual issue published in 3 vols.
   7. Issues for 1981 published in 2 vols.
   8. Issue for May 1957 issued in 2 pts.; pt. 2 bears former title.
   9. 1979-1981 issued in 2 pts., with pt. 2 on microfiche.
   10. Two pts. to a vol., each pt. with special t.p. and, in v. 1-2, 99, 105, 114 with separate paging.
   11. Beginning 1974 each edition published in more than one vol.

12. Each supplement issued in several vols.
13. Some issues appear in more than 1 fascicle.
14. Some issues issued in 2 or more vols.
15. Each cumulation published in 4 or more vols.
16. Issues for <1979-> published in 2 or more unnumbered vols.
17. Proceedings for <1978>-1985 issued in two or more pts.
18. Vols. for <1/4/1979-30/6/1979> issued in pts. each covering a different topic.
19. Vols. for 1968-   published in several issues, each issue covering one county.
20. Issued in pts. continuously paged and supplied with a general t.p. and subject index to form a vol.
21. Each issue consists of multiple discs.
22. Additional discs distributed monthly; number of discs in each distribution varies.
23. Issues consist of an Installation Disk and a Data Disk.
24. Monthly installments issued on 2 computer disks.
25. Each v. issued on 2 high-density 1.4Mb or 4 double-density 800K disks.

E. Multiple or revised editions
   1. Each vol. issued in multiple editions.
   2. Some vols. issued in revised editions.
   3. Vols. for 1981-   called Revised.
   4. Vol. for 1978 issued in a revised ed., Aug. 1979.
   5. Vols. for FY 1982 issued in 2 sets, the second being a revised edition.
   6. Subsequent issues of each vol. constitute revisions of previous ones, which they supersede.
   7. Issued in alternating Japanese and European editions with even no. being Japanese and describing Japanese cars and the odd no. being European, describing European cars.

F. Cumulations (For cumulations issued under separate title, see "580 Linking Entry Complexity Note.")
   1. Each issue is cumulative.
   2. One issue per month cumulates previous month's weekly issues.
   3. Vols. for   -1977/80, 1981-   are cumulative.
   4. Only cumulative annual issue published for 1980.
   5. Each issue cumulates the preceding year for a period of up to five years.

6. Issues for Dec. 1973 and Dec. 1974 cumulate issues for the preceding year; issue no. 42 (June 1976), called also v. 3, cumulates issues published Jan. 1975-May 1976; issues for fall 1976-spring 1977 called v. 4, no. 1-3.
7. <1982>-1989, the Dec. issue is cumulative for the year.
8. The June issue, called 1. Halbjahr, cumulates Jan.-May; the Dec. issue, called Jahresband, cumulates Jan.-Nov.
9. Each issues cumulates the entire set.
10. Issues are cumulative, with backfile disks issued periodically.
11. Began with the simultaneous release in summer 1989 of annual cumulations for the years 1986 through 1988 and the 2nd quarter cumulation for Jan.-June 1989; quarterly issues thereafter are cumulative, with the fourth issue each year comprising the final archival cumulation. Beginning 1990, retrospective cumulations for <-1985> released, as available, in reverse chronological order.

PRELIMINARY ISSUES

1. Charter issue published in 1978.
2. Pre-publication issue published July 1980.
3. An introductory number was issued as Test number 0-1978.
4. Issue for spring 1982, called also "Premier issue," lacks numbering but constitutes vol. 1, no. 1.
5. Vol. 1, no. 1 preceded by three "experimental issues."
6. A "prototype issue" called v. 1, no. 0 was issued Oct. 16, 1978.
7. Vol. 1, no. 1 preceded by unnumbered, undated prototype issue.
8. Vol. 1, no. 1, preceded by an issue numbered v. 1, no. 1 and called: Prospectus 1968.
9. Vol. 1, no. 1 preceded by a number dated Dec. 1965 called Subscription issue.
10. Vol. 1, no.1 preceded by a number dated July/Dec. 1975, and a transitional volume dated May 1973-June 1975.
11. Vol. 1, no. 1 preceded by a sample issue called also v. no. 1 and dated Nov. 15, 1977.
12. Vol. 0, published 1972, covers periodical literature published from 1954 until the issuance of vol. 1 in 1964.
13. Preceded by an issue called: Demo, Vol. 0.

SUSPENSION OF PUBLICATION

1. Suspended with v. 10, 1917 and resumed with New ser., v. 1 (Dec. 1924).
2. Suspended following its May 1969 issue. Resumed with Jan. 1970 issue.
3. Publication was temporarily suspended with no. 2, May-June 1963; resumed with July 1966 issue.
4. Suspended 1962-72; a four volume set covering 1962-72 was published in 1976.
    ✦ [AACR2R: 1962-1972]
5. Suspended <1863>-Apr. 1866.

ITEMS NOT PUBLISHED

1. None published 1974.
2. No issue published for 1979.
3. Not published Mar.-Dec. 1973.
4. No separate issue published for 1977-78.
    ✦ [AACR2R: 1977-1978]
5. No numbers issued for Sept. 1914-July 1915 and 1944.
6. No conference records published before 1978.
7. No proceedings published for the first 5 conferences.
8. Proceedings of the 1st-66th meetings not published.
9. No annuals published for 1940-1946? when the academy was merged with the Accademia d'Italia.
10. Issues for 1948-1958 which constitute v. 26-34 not published.
11. No. 49-50 announced but never published.
12. Vols. 1-33 not published. Adopts its numbering from Bulletin signalétique and its continuations.

TYPE OF COMPUTER FILE OR DATA NOTE

DEFINITION/SCOPE

OCLC Bibliographic Formats and Standards, 2nd ed.:
Notes that characterize the file. In addition to a general descriptor (e.g., text, computer program, numeric), use field 516 for specific form or genre data (e.g., biography, dictionaries, indexes).

CONSER Editing Guide, 1994 ed.:
Record information that characterizes computer file aspects of a serial in field 516. More specific information, such as the format or genre of the serial files (e.g., ASCII, hypertext, electronic journal), may be included along with a general description (e.g., text and graphic files).

Field 516 does not end with a mark of punctuation unless the field ends with an abbreviation, initial/letter, or other data that ends with a mark of punctuation.

---

1. Hypertext (electronic journal)
2. Electronic serial in ASCII text, and HTML format vol. 4-
3. Electronic newsletter available in ASCII text and in hypertext
4. Written in ISO 9660 format
5. Disc characteristics: CD-ROM (ISO 9660 standard)
6. Electronic journal in Chinese text
7. Electronic newspaper
8. Contains graphic art samples in TIFF & EPS file formats for use with several popular desktop publishing layout, draw, and paint application programs
9. Available in two ASCII versions, paginated and running text; RTF ("Rich text format" readable by MS-Word and other word processors for both DOS & Mac); MS Word 4.0/Mac (binary); and WordPerfect 5.1 (binary)
10. Available in three "desktop editions" that can be downloaded and printed in Acrobat, PageMaker, and WordPerfect formats. Also in ASCII format
11. Statistical data analysis program

DATE/TIME AND PLACE OF AN EVENT NOTE

DEFINITION/SCOPE

OCLC Bibliographic Formats and Standards, 2nd ed.:
The capture date and place (i.e., the date/time and/or place of a recording, filming, execution, broadcast, or in the case of a naturally occurring object, of finding). Use field 033 to enter this data in coded form.

Because this note is not generally used in serial records, it is not defined in *CONSER Editing Guide*, 1994 ed.

SUMMARY, ETC. NOTE

DEFINITION/SCOPE

OCLC Bibliographic Formats and Standards, 2nd ed.:
A summary, abstract, annotation, and other types of similar notes. Use also for formal summary statements that would be preceded by the word *summary* or for other informal statements.

CONSER Editing Guide, 1994 ed.:
Field 520 contains unformatted notes describing the scope and contents of the work. For serials, this note is limited to formal summary statements preceded by the term "Summary."

Informal summary notes are recorded in field 500. Notes that cite a related publication are recorded in field 580.

✦ Editors' note: The examples are shown without the print constant "Summary:".

1. Provides summaries of articles as well as the full text of its classified job notices appearing in the corresponding issue of the Chronicle of higher education.
2. Index of periodicals on architecture, 1978- ; books, exhibition catalogs, and technical reports catalogued by the British Architectural Library, 1984- ; and audio visual materials acquired by the Library.
3. Artikelbasen på CD-ROM indexes larger articles from 8 nationwide Danish newspapers and approximately 800 current Danish periodicals and annual publications from 1981 to the present.
4. Newsletter concerning the systematics of the Leguminosae/Fabaceae.
5. No. 1-13 are short-term studies; with no. 14 becomes a series of supplementary reports summarizing the results of longer term data collection.

6. Provides full text images of the annual reports issued by over 10,000 non-US public companies in 100 countries.
7. Provides abstracts and full-text access to printed articles. Excludes: advertisements, dividend tables, digests of earnings tables, futures prices, and stock tables and other free-standing tabular material. Articles printed in 1990 and after include section and page numbers.
8. "IP magazine features articles on the latest and most controversial developments in the laws governing technology and information—from federal copyright law to the protection of trade secrets to antitrust enforcement"—Introductory page.
9. Database of European law firms with search capabilities allowing for the selection of law firms meeting designated criteria.
10. The focus of the journal is on current legal issues in judicial decisions, law reform, legislation, legal research, policy related socio-legal research, and information technology and practice.
11. Indexed full-text electronic version of articles, editorials, and reviews found in the print version of the periodical.
12. "Internet Lyme disease information source."
13. Contains references to articles published in Hungarian and international newspapers and periodicals (full-text not included).
14. U.S. Geological Survey daily values and peak values for all U.S.G.S. station gauges from their inception. Data cover stream flows, lake levels, water quality (including well water) and meteorology for U.S. Programs support manipulation, storage, and printing in ASCII table format, Lotus 1-2-3, card image, and binary.
15. "Facsimile images of United States patents"—Disc label.
16. Provides access to fulltext transcripts of television news programs produced by NBC News.

TARGET AUDIENCE NOTE

DEFINITION/SCOPE

OCLC Bibliographic Formats and Standards, 2nd ed.:
Note that describes the target audience of the item. The target audience is the persons, institutions, or individuals for whom the item is intended. Use field 521 if different versions, editions, or distributions exist with different contents or annotations.

If both reading grade and interest age or grade level data is present in field 521, enter codes in *Audn* based on interest age or grade information.

If the note is about restrictions on access, use field 506.

CONSER Editing Guide, 1994 ed.:
Field 521 contains information about the users or the intended audience of the material described. In CONSER records, this field is limited to quoted notes describing the intended audience of the publication.

1. "Catholic paper for the Slovaks in Cleveland, Ohio and vicinity."
2. "For use by employers located in the Province of Quebec."
3. "The national gay newsmagazine."

GEOGRAPHIC COVERAGE NOTE

DEFINITION/SCOPE

OCLC Bibliographic Formats and Standards, 2nd ed.:
Notes about the geographic coverage of the item (usually for survey material). Use field 043 or 052 for geographic data in coded form.

CONSER Editing Guide, 1994 ed.:
Field 522 is used to record the geographic coverage of the serial. The coded form of the geographic information is recorded in field 052 (Geographic Classification Code).

1. Eastern United States; gauge station level, by state.
2. County-level data from four Northwestern states (Washington, Oregon, Idaho, Montana)

TIME PERIOD OF CONTENT NOTE (OBSOLETE)

DEFINITION/SCOPE

"This computer files field was made obsolete because, according to the guidelines agreed upon for separate notes, its continued existence could not be justified. The information can be recorded in field 500 (General Note), in subfield b (Period covered) of field 513 (Type of Report and Period Covered Note), or in field 518 (Date/Time and Place of an Event Note)"—*Format Integration and Its Effect on the USMARC Bibliographic Format*, 1995 ed.

OCLC Bibliographic Formats and Standards, 2nd ed.:
Field 523 was used for notes about the time period covered by the contents of the file and/or the dates when the data was collected. Use field 500 for time period of content notes. Use field 045 for date information in coded form.

PREFERRED CITATION OF DESCRIBED MATERIALS NOTE

DEFINITION/SCOPE

OCLC Bibliographic Formats and Standards, 2nd ed.:
Note about the custodian's preferred citation of the described materials.

Because this note is not generally used in serial records, it is not defined in *CONSER Editing Guide*, 1994 ed.

SUPPLEMENT NOTE

DEFINITION/SCOPE

OCLC Bibliographic Formats and Standards, 2nd ed.:
Notes that clarify or amplify any supplement or special issue rela-
tionship that is **not** in a separate record or in linking entry field 770.
Use also for unnamed supplements and/or special issues.

CONSER Editing Guide, 1994 ed.:
Field 525 records the issuance of supplements or special issues not
input as separate records (and, therefore, not recorded in field 770).
Field 525 is used primarily for unnamed supplements and/or special
issues, but named supplements that are not cataloged on a separate
record may also be mentioned.

◆ Editors' note: For named supplements published separately, see "580 Linking
Entry Complexity Note."

UNNAMED SUPPLEMENTS

1. Has some supplements.
2. Has occasional supplements.
3. Some issues include supplements.
4. Some numbers issued with supplements.
5. Each vol. includes supplements for the previous years.
6. Includes occasional unnumbered supplements.
7. Includes occasional consecutively numbered supplementary
   issues.
8. Includes supplements and extraordinary issues.
9. Unpaged supplements accompany some numbers.
10. Separately paged supplements accompany some numbers.

11. Statistical supplements accompany some reports.
12. Some issues contain supplements on special topics.
13. Supplements accompany vols. for 1971 and 1973.
14. Vol. 5-   accompanied by supplements issued in alternate years.
15. Supplements issued at intervals of two months.
16. Supplements published every July and Jan.
17. Includes an annual supplement.
18. Supplements issued between some editions.
19. Some issues accompanied by separately paged supplements and sections consisting principally of convention proceedings, and list of members and branch societies.
20. Issues for 1952-   accompanied by supplement containing summaries of each article in English, French, and German.
21. Some issues for <1972-> accompanied by supplementary material on microfiche.
22. Has separately issued support documents reproduced on microfiche.
23. IDF standards and documents issued as supplements.
24. Uncumulated abstracts and indices issued as supplements.
25. The issues for 1977 and 1978 constitute the first and second supplements to the 1976 issue.
26. Supplements have been issued since 1929 (Archives v. 7, no. 1) and bear parallel numbering to the "cahiers" of the archives.
27. Sept. 1996 issue supplemented by CD-ROM containing full-text of 9th National Conference on Synchrotron Radiation Instrumentation.
28. Some issues for <1973-> accompanied by supplementary material on microfiche; <1995-> by supporting information on microfiche.

NAMED SUPPLEMENTS NOT PUBLISHED SEPARATELY

(For named supplements published separately, see "580 Linking Entry Complexity Note.")

1. Supplements with title: TV supplément accompany each number.
2. Index for v. 1-20 (1947-66) also called its Supplementary publication, no. 3.
    ✦ [AACR2R: 1947-1966]

3. Separately paged supplements called Section 2 with title Trends and patterns accompany each number.
4. Vols. for 1950-<1952> accompanied by a supplementary report, dated July, with title: The midyear economic report.
5. First ed. accompanied by 2 supplements: suppl. 1, Additions, revisions, and labor unions; suppl. 2, Functional and topical listings.
6. No. 12 (July 1980) has a supplement dated July 1981 and called Research series, supplement.
7. Sept. 1994 issue supplemented by CD-ROM: Medical multimedia informatics.
8. Sept. 1996 issue supplemented by CD-ROM containing full-text of 9th National Conference on Synchrotron Radiation Instrumentation.

SPECIAL ISSUES

1. Special issues accompany some no.
2. Some issues appear as special editions.
3. Some numbers are published as Monograph/special issues.
4. Some issues have no vol. numbering, but are called Special issue.
5. An industry reference guide is published annually as part of the publishing frequency of Landscape & turf industry.
6. Includes special releases.

UPDATES

(For updates that are not supplements, see "500 General Note"; for named updates, see "580 Linking Entry Complexity Note.")

✦ Editors' note: Up-to-date should have hyphens.

1. Editions kept up-to-date by midyear supplements.
2. Quarterly updating supplements are issued between editions.
3. Has quarterly supplements for 1973.
4. Updating supplements published April, July, and October.
5. Kept up-to-date with supplemental sheets.
6. Kept up to date, 1980-198 , by supplement called: FAA airworthiness directive; <1991-> Large aircraft kept up to date by: FAA airworthiness directives. Large aircraft. Book 2; and

Small aircraft and rotorcraft kept up to date by: FAA airworthiness directives. Small aircraft and rotorcraft. Book 2.

7. Kept up-to-date by supplementary bulletins issued twice monthly.
8. Updated by irregular supplements which are combined annually with cumulative indexes.
9. Vols. for 1981-   kept up-to-date with an annual cross-referenced supplement.
10. Kept up to date 1963-1972 by semi-annual supplements covering all pts.; from 1973? each pt. is kept up to date by a cumulated supplement.
11. Updates issued from time to time are called supplements.
12. Kept up to date during the year by occasional supplements <1981-1984>; kept up to date by supplement <1986-1987->

ACCOMPANYING INFORMATION

1. Addendum accompany some numbers.
2. First biennial report provides an overview. A more detailed document issued as an Addendum.
3. Technical appendixes accompany some numbers.
4. Accompanied each year by separate reports on various areas.
5. Vols. for 1981-   accompanied by narrative statements of federal courts in separately published appendices.
6. Vols. for <1978-> accompanied by map in pocket.
7. Vols. for <1981-> accompanied by folded color map.
8. Issue for Sept. 1980 accompanied by sound recording.
9. Vol. 96, no. 4 has appendix on CD-ROM.
10. Special issues accompanied by CD-ROM, <vol. 39, no. 3>

CENSORSHIP NOTE (OBSOLETE)

DEFINITION/SCOPE

"This visual materials field was made obsolete because according to the guidelines agreed upon for separate notes its continued existence could not be justified; the information can be recorded in field 500 (General Note)"—*Format Integration and Its Effect on the USMARC Bibliographic Format*, 1995 ed.

ADDITIONAL PHYSICAL FORM AVAILABLE NOTE

DEFINITION/SCOPE

OCLC Bibliographic Formats and Standards, 2nd ed.:
Notes about a different physical format in which the described item is available. If the publisher of the additional physical form is different from the publisher of the item being cataloged, enter source and order number information for the additional form. The additional form may be published and/or made available for use at a repository in the additional form. When specific title and data base control number information are available for the other format, enter the title and control number in field 776 (Additional Physical Form Entry).

Information in field 530 is usually taken from the original item.

Use only for notes describing different physical formats. Enter notes conveying information about other editions (e.g., earlier versions, shorter versions, different language versions) in field 500 (General note).

If the work is a reprint (regular, eye-readable print), use field 260 for reprint information and describe the original work in field 580.

CONSER Editing Guide, 1994 ed.:
Field 530 may be used on a record for the original item to note the existence of one or more reproductions or versions in different physical formats. Information given in field 530 is usually taken from the original item. When a linking entry field is given in conjunction with field 530, it is tagged 776.

1. Available in a concurrent microfiche ed.
2. Also issued on microfiche.
3. Issued also on microfiche simultaneously with the paper edition and on microfilm at end of subscription year.
4. Available on microfilm from Xerox University Microfilms.
5. Available on microfilm from Johnson Associates, Inc., University Microfilms, and Princeton Microfilms.
6. Also available in 16 mm. microfilm.
7. Available also in microfiche, which includes supplementary material.
8. Vols. for <Jan.-Dec. 1981-> distributed to depository libraries in microfiche.
9. Issued also in a print ed.
10. Issued also in paper format version.
11. Also available online via Wilsonline.
12. Issued also in print format as: Journal of artificial intelligence research.
13. Issued also on microfiche and computer diskette.
14. Online version of the print publication.
15. Online version of: Emerging infectious diseases (Print).
16. Also available on CD-ROM with title: U.S. Supreme Court reports, L Ed.
17. CD-ROM ed. of: United States. Supreme Court. Cases argued and decided in the Supreme Court of the United States (Lawyers' edition); and: United States. Supreme Court. United States Supreme Court reports.
18. CD-ROM version of: Architectural periodicals index, 1978-1994; Architectural publications index, 1995-
19. Also available through electronic bulletin board TAXACOM.
20. CSD database also available as a tape-loaded database.
21. Also issued on computer tape from the International Monetary Fund.

REPRODUCTION NOTE

DEFINITION/SCOPE

OCLC Bibliographic Formats and Standards, 2nd ed.:
Notes that describe items that are reproductions of original materials. Base the bibliographic description on the original publication. Describe the reproduction in a note.

CONSER Editing Guide, 1994 ed.:
Field 533 is used to describe a reproduction of a serial when the description is based on the original. Field 533 is most commonly used for reproduction microforms (Cf. LCRI Chapter 11).

Input field 533 as the last 5XX field, following 5XX fields that relate to the original. (Optional field 539 may follow field 533.)

Field 533 may be given in AACR2 form, regardless of whether the description for the original item is AACR2 or pre-AACR2.

1. Microfilm. Ann Arbor, Mich. : Xerox University Microfilms. microfilm reels ; 35 mm. (Current periodical series).
2. Microfiche. Cambridge, England : Chadwyck-Healey Ltd. ; Teaneck, N.J. : Somerset House, 1977. microfiche sheets ; 10 x 15 cm. (European official statistical serials on microfiche).
3. Microfiche. Ann Arbor, Mich. : University Microfilms International, 1979- sheets ; 11 x 15 cm. (Current periodical series ; pub. no. 2203.).

ORIGINAL VERSION NOTE

DEFINITION/SCOPE

OCLC Bibliographic Formats and Standards, 2nd ed.:
Notes about map facsimiles and certain graphic materials (e.g., a poster reproduction of a painting) when you are cataloging according to AACR2, rule 1.11A, and/or *Cartographic Materials*, section 11. Both prescribe that you describe such reproductions in the body of the record, and enter details about the original in a note. Preface details about the original with a standard introductory phrase such as *Original version*:

Use field 534 for VIS and MAP only. The Library of Congress and OCLC have adopted the policy of AACR1 (i.e., to describe the original in the body of the record, and enter a note for the reproduction) for cataloging reproductions for all other formats.

CONSER Editing Guide, 1994 ed.:
Field 534 contains information about the original publication when the record in hand describes a photoreproduction, a facsimile, or a microform reproduction. Details relevant to the original are given in field 534 when they differ from the information describing the reproduction.

For serials, field 534 is used for microforms cataloged by the National Library of Canada. Other CONSER members use field 533 for microforms to cite the details of the microform (according to the provisions of LCRI Chapter 11) and field 580 for reprints to cite the details of the original.

Field 534 is used in conjunction with fields 530 and 776.

1. Reproduction of: Ontario ed. Toronto.
2. Original published: Halifax, N.S. : W. Armand.
3. Original published: Winnipeg : Manitoba Teachers' Foundation. Issued by the federation under its later name: Manitoba Teachers' Society, 1942-

LOCATION OF ORIGINALS/ DUPLICATES NOTE

DEFINITION/SCOPE

OCLC Bibliographic Formats and Standards, 2nd ed.:
Note for the name of the repository with custody over originals or duplicates. Use also to identify holders of the original collection, a duplicate collection, or an oral tape collection.

Use field 535 if the originals or duplicates are housed in a repository different from that of the materials in hand.

CONSER Editing Guide, 1994 ed.:
Use field 535 to record the name and address of the repository with custody over originals or duplicates of the described materials. This field is used only when the originals or duplicates are housed in a repository different from that of the materials being described.

1. Coal reports. American Mining Congress; 1920 N. St., NW, Washington, D.C. 20036; 202-861-2800
2. Company histories U.S. Army Military History Institute; Carlisle Barracks, PA 17013; 717-245-3601, 3434 pau

FUNDING INFORMATION NOTE

DEFINITION/SCOPE

OCLC Bibliographic Formats and Standards, 2nd ed.:
Notes about contract, grant names, and project numbers if the material results from a funded project.

Because this note is not generally used in serial records, it is not defined in *CONSER Editing Guide*, 1994 ed.

SOURCE OF DATA NOTE (OBSOLETE)

DEFINITION/SCOPE

"This computer files field was made obsolete because according to the guidelines agreed upon for separate notes its continued existence could not be justified. The information can be recorded in field 500 (General Note) or included in field 567 (Methodology Note)"— *Format Integration and Its Effect on the USMARC Bibliographic Format,* 1995 ed.

SYSTEM DETAILS NOTE

DEFINITION/SCOPE

OCLC Bibliographic Formats and Standards, 2nd ed.:
Notes for the system information for the item. Such information includes the presence or absence of certain kinds of codes or the physical characteristics of a computer file such as recording densities, parity, or blocking factors.

For software, enter data such as software programming language, computer requirements (e.g., computer manufacturer and model, operating system, or memory requirements), and peripheral requirements (e.g., number of tape drives, number of disk or drum units, number of terminals, or other peripherals devices, support software or related equipment).

For videorecordings, enter information about the trade name or recording systems(s) (VHS, Beta, etc.), number of lines of resolution, and modulation frequency.

CONSER Editing Guide, 1994 ed.:
Record system information in field 538 for the following types of serials:
- Direct access computer files
- Remote access computer files
- Videorecordings

"System requirements" information for computer files, such as software programming language, computer requirements (e.g., computer manufacturer and model, operating system, or memory requirements), and peripheral requirements (e.g., number of disks, support software, or related equipment) can be included for computer file serials. System requirements for "electronic serials," in addition to those necessary for standard Internet access, may also be specified.

"Mode of access" information for computer file serials available by remote access should also be recorded in field 538. It may be appropriate to include different types of information specified by AACR2 9.7B1 (Nature and scope and system requirements) in a single note.

For serial videorecordings, information about the trade name or recording systems(s) (VHS, Beta, etc.), number of lines of resolution, and modulation frequency may be recorded.

SYSTEM REQUIREMENTS

1. System requirements: PC; 430 kilobytes available memory; DOS 3.1 or later; ISO 9660-compatible CD-ROM reader.
2. System requirements: IBM-PC or compatible; 512K (560K to run VGA graphics); CD-ROM player with Microsoft extensions and compatible driver; 360K free disk space; VGA adapter and monitor (optional).
3. System requirements: IBM PC/XT/AT/386/486 or 100% compatible computers; 640K of RAM; MS-DOS version 3.2 or higher.
4. System requirements: IBM PC 286, 386, 486, PS/2, or compatible with at least 640K RAM (450K free); hard disk with at least 2Mb free; Hercules monochrome, EGA or VGA monitor, CD-ROM drive and controller card with Microsoft CD-ROM 2.1 or higher.
5. Equipment requirement: Chinese system software on PC/Windows, Macintosh, Unix, X-Window or VMS for viewing GB, HZ, Big5 encoded Chinese characters; or a graphic viewer for gif format images.

MODE OF ACCESS

1. Mode of access: Internet email; contact publisher for subscription laws@ai.sri.com.
2. Mode of access: World Wide Web (URL: http://www.jstor.org/journals/00223808.html).

3. Mode of access: Internet email, telnet, gopher, and World Wide Web. For email subscription, send to: listserv@loc.gov, the message: subscribe consrlin [firstname lastname].

4. Mode of access: Electronic mail, FTP, gopher, telnet, and World Wide Web. For email subscription, send to: listserv@library.berkeley.edu, the message: sub cites [first name last name]. For telnet access, telnet to MELVYL.UCOP.EDU and enter the command: SHOW CURRENT CITES. Also distributed on the PACS-L and PACS-P lists. Issues are also accessible via the CICNet Electronic Journals Collection via the World Wide Web (URL: http://ejournals.cic.net/entry.5.html).

5. Mode of access: Electronic mail, dial-in, gopher, and World Wide Web. For email subscription, send to: listproc@lists.colorado.edu, the message: SUBSCRIBE HAZARDS [first name last name].

6. Dial-in access available on the following bulletin board systems: State and Local Emergency Management Data Users Group (SALEMDUG) at (708) 739-1312; VITANET BBS, (703) 527-1086; Colorado HazardNet BBS, (303) 465-5013; and: Safety Connection (SAFNet), (801) 831-4351, FIDO 1:3003/911 or 1:3003/913.

7. Mode of access: ASCII files via FTP from dla.ucop.edu in the directory /usr/users/ftp/pub/dla/bulletin.

VIDEORECORDINGS

1. Videocassettes in Beta II format.
2. Available in both Beta and VHS formats.
3. Compact disc.

TERMS GOVERNING USE AND REPRODUCTION NOTE

DEFINITION/SCOPE

OCLC Bibliographic Formats and Standards, 2nd ed.:
Notes for rules about using the materials after the holder grants access. Use for copyrights, film rights, trade restrictions, etc. that restrict the right to reproduce, exhibit, fictionalize, or quote.

If the note is about restriction on access, use field 506.

Because this note is not generally used in serial records, it is not defined in *CONSER Editing Guide*, 1994 ed.

IMMEDIATE SOURCE OF ACQUISITION NOTE

DEFINITION/SCOPE

OCLC Bibliographic Formats and Standards, 2nd ed.:
Note naming the immediate source of acquisition. Use primarily for original or historical items, or other archival collections.

For notes about the original source of acquisition, use field 561.

Because this note is not generally used in serial records, it is not defined in *CONSER Editing Guide*, 1994 ed.

LOCATION OF ASSOCIATED ARCHIVAL MATERIALS NOTE

DEFINITION/SCOPE

OCLC Bibliographic Formats and Standards, 2nd ed.:
Note for the name and address of the custodian of manuscripts and archival materials related to the materials by provenance, that is, by having been a part of the same collection or record group (not reproductions, published versions, or studies based on the materials).

Because this note is not generally used in serial records, it is not defined in *CONSER Editing Guide*, 1994 ed.

BIOGRAPHICAL OR HISTORICAL NOTE

DEFINITION/SCOPE

OCLC Bibliographic Formats and Standards, 2nd ed.:
Biographic or historical notes about the main entry. Use for notes about the life of a person, the history of an institution, or about an event.

Because this note is not generally used in serial records, it is not defined in *CONSER Editing Guide*, 1994 ed.

LANGUAGE NOTE

DEFINITION/SCOPE

OCLC Bibliographic Formats and Standards, 2nd ed.:
Note about the languages of the text. Associate notes with codes in *Lang* and field 041. Use also for notes about systems of words and grammar, including natural languages and their dialects and artificial languages (e.g., data processing languages). Use also for notes about distinctive alphabets or symbol systems.

CONSER Editing Guide, 1994 ed.:
Field 546 provides information concerning the language or languages of the text, summaries, etc.

LANGUAGE OF TEXT

(For notes concerning language of title/parallel title information, see "500 General Note.")

1. Papers published in any language.
2. Text is multilingual (romanized).
3. Entries in English and Chinese.
4. Text in English, German, and other languages.
5. Portuguese, Chinese, and English.
6. French, Mar./June 1981- ; Dutch and French, <Dec. 1981>
7. Text in English only.
8. Text in English; comparative tables in English and French.
9. Includes some text in French.
10. Chiefly in Italian with occasional contributions in German.
11. Text in English; includes some textual material in other European languages.

12. Articles primarily in Dutch, some in English.
13. In French or in various other languages with French translation.
14. In English and French, with French text on inverted pages.
15. Text in English and French, 1972- ; French text on inverted pages, 1976/1977-
16. Reports for the years <, 1975/76-> have parallel texts in German and English.
17. Text in English and French, each with special t.p. and separate paging. French text on inverted pages.
18. No. 1-5 contain parallel texts in French and English; no. 6- available in either English or French editions.
19. Issues for <1995:1-> no longer published in Greek.
20. Search interface in English, Dutch, French, German, Italian, and Spanish.
21. Main menus in Dutch and French; search screens in Dutch, English, French, German, and Spanish.
22. In Azerbaijani (Arabic script).

LANGUAGE OF SUMMARY, ETC.

1. Some summaries in English and French.
2. Text in German or English; English summaries.
3. Text in Polish; summaries in English, Russian, or Spanish.
4. In Chinese and Japanese; with summaries in Chinese, English, and Japanese.
5. Early issues include English and French summaries of selected articles.
6. Articles in English, French, or German; summaries in all three languages.
7. Text in Dutch and English, the former with summaries in English.
8. Turkish and English; each article accompanied by a summary in the other language.
9. Articles in English and French with summaries in the alternate language.
10. Articles in French and English with summaries in one or both of these languages.
11. English or French, with summaries in the other language and in Spanish or German.
12. Portuguese, with some articles in English; summaries in English and French.

13. Text in German and French; tables of contents also in Polish and Russian; summaries in Polish and Russian.
14. Articles largely in Japanese, some in English; some tables of contents and summaries in English.
15. Articles mainly in English with some in French and Italian; summaries in English, French, German, Italian, and Spanish.
16. German articles with summaries or abstracts in English; English articles with summaries or abstracts in German; some French.
17. Tables of contents also in French; summaries in French and English.
18. Some vols. are accompanied by a separately paged summary in French and English.

TRANSLATION INFORMATION

(For general translation information, see "500 General Note.")

1. In Portuguese, with the second half of the issue being the English translation.
2. French translation of Chinese articles, with summaries in English and French.
3. Multilingual; foreign language contributions usually with English translation.

FORMER TITLE COMPLEXITY NOTE

DEFINITION/SCOPE

OCLC Bibliographic Formats and Standards, 2nd ed.:
Pre-AACR2 latest entry cataloging only.

Use for a "title varies" note that is so complex that an intelligible note cannot be provided by the 247 print constant (i.e., *Title varies:*). If a note is present in field 547, enter the former titles in separate 247 fields. Do not use this field for successive entry cataloging.

CONSER Editing Guide, 1994 ed.:
According to CONSER policy, field 547 is used only in the following situations: 1) records for reproduction microforms that have been "cloned" from a latest entry record for the original serial; and 2) records created from preexisting cataloging when performing retrospective conversion. Field 547 is not used in current AACR2 cataloging records.

1. Title varies: 1716?-1858, Notizie del mondo; 1860-71, 1912- Annuario pontificio (1872-1911, Gerarchia cattolica).
2. Title varies: <1951/52-1961/62> Costa's tobacco directory of the United States and of the world. Annuarie universal des tabacs. Directorio universal de tabacos.

ISSUING BODY NOTE

DEFINITION/SCOPE

OCLC Bibliographic Formats and Standards, 2nd ed.:
Note that refers to current and former issuing bodies, including notes containing editing, compiling, or translating information that involves an issuing body.

Use for notes denoting the item as an official organ of a society, etc.

Use for issuing bodies traced in a 7XX added entry. The field explains their relationship to the publication and justified the 7XX added entry.

If the note is about a commercial publisher, use field 500.

CONSER Editing Guide, 1994 ed.:
Field 550 refers to current and former issuing bodies. Field 500 is generally used for issuing bodies traced in a 7XX added entry field. The field explains their relationship to the publication and justifies the 7XX added entries. Notes relating to commercial publishers, distributors, or places of publication are tagged 500.

GENERAL ISSUING BODY NOTES

1. Issued by: Pennsylvania State Library, Oct. 1963-Mar. 1971; State Library of Pennsylvania, May 1971-
2. Earlier vols. issued by Alabama Dept. of Public Health, Special Services Administration, Division of Vital Statistics.
3. Second quarter 1979- issued jointly with Bureau of Industrial Economics.
4. Vol. for 1979 issued with: Oficina de Planificación Agricola.

5. Sponsored by Region 5, of the Institute of Electrical and Electronics Engineers, 1976; and by other sections of the Institute, 1977-

6. No. 2-3 (May 1981)- sponsored jointly by the International Funds for the Promotion of Culture of UNESCO and by EACROTANAL.

7. Developed by: the Library, and Information Services Division, Environmental Science Information Center.

8. Proceedings compiled by the ARC Weed Research Organization.

9. Compiled and edited by the Cataloging Publication Division, Library of Congress.

10. 2nd- report prepared by the Dept.'s Bureau of Automotive Repair.

11. Prepared for the annual meeting with the assistance and cooperation of the Gulf Coast Section of the Society of Economic Paleontologists and Mineralogists, 1954-

12. Produced by: students at San Diego State University.

13. Produced in cooperation with Burwood State College.

14. Measured in cooperation with: the Arkansas Geological Commission.

15. Founded by the Central Ontario Industrial Relations Institute and now published in co-operation with the Office of Arbitration, Ontario Ministry of Labour.

16. Vols. for -1980 approved by the World Food and Agricultural Outlook and Situation Board.

17. Digitized and made available by: Project Muse.

18. Issued in its electronic form by the Scholarly Communications Project of Virginia Tech.

19. "The journal is managed by graduate students throughout the United States and Canada and is electronically transmitted via the Adult Education Network (AEDNET), accessible through BITNET and Internet."

20. Citations selected from the National Library of Medicine's MEDLINE database.

21. Database made available through the Waste Management Information Bureau of AEA Environment & Energy.

PUBLISHER INFORMATION

(For imprint variation notes, see "500 General Note.")

1. Published as a trial research project by the Program Evaluation Resource Center.
2. Vols. for 1965-19   published by Asian Peoples' Anti-Communist League.
3. Vols. published in Berlin "herausgegeben" by R. Fischer; in Wrocław issued by Uniwersytet Wrocławski im. Bolesława Bieruta.
4. Published by the Music Section of the Department of Cultural Affairs of the Pan American Union, to complement the more extensive Boletin interamericano de Música published by the Section in Spanish.
5. No. 1 (fall 1970) published in association with Stony Brook Poetics Foundation; New ser. Vol. 1, no. 1-v. 4, no. 2 published by Boston University.
6. Published under the auspices of the Rutgers Institute of Jazz Studies, 1982-
7. Published under the auspices of: Gesellschaft Deutscher Chemiker, Deutsche Gesellschaft für Chemisches Apparatewesen, VDI-Gesellschaft Verfahrenstechnik und Chemieingenieurwesen (GVC).
8. Some numbers also published by Colorado Dept. of Health.
9. Published with the support of the International Association of Hotel Management Schools.
10. Quarterly publication of the Stalnaker Family Association, Oct. 1979-
11. Published for the International Society for Test Anxiety Research, 1982-
12. Published on behalf of the Faculty of Law, University of Oxford.

OFFICIAL ORGAN, PUBLICATION, ETC.

1. Official journal of: Forest Industry Engineering Association and the Timber Machinists Educational Association.
2. Official magazine of the Southern Rhodesia Tourist Board, July/Aug. 1964-Sept./Oct. 1964; of Rhodesia National Tourist Board, Nov./Dec. 1964-Mar./Apr. 1965.
3. Official publication of the National Society for Performance and Instruction.

4. Beginning with Jan. 1941, issued as the bulletin of the Société de géographie.
5. Service to members of Computists International.

VARIANT NAMES

1. Vols. for Jan. 1979- issued under the Office of Administration's new name, the Office of Management and Agency Services.
2. Issued 1975-1977 by Research Section, Dept. of Health and Social Development (called 1978-1979, Dept. of Health and Community Services).
3. Issuing body varies slightly: Skipjack Programme.
4. Vols. for <1995-> published under the later name of the section: Law and Courts Section.

ENTITY AND ATTRIBUTE NOTE

DEFINITION/SCOPE

OCLC Bibliographic Formats and Standards, 2nd ed.:
Notes for descriptions of the information content of the data set, including the entity types, their attributes, and the domains from which attribute values may be assigned.

Because this note is not generally used in serial records, it is not defined in *CONSER Editing Guide*, 1994 ed.

CUMULATIVE INDEX/ FINDING AIDS NOTE

DEFINITION/SCOPE

OCLC Bibliographic Formats and Standards, 2nd ed.:
Note identifying the availability of cumulative indexes and/or finding aids whose only or major focus is the described material. Use field 510 (Citation/References Note) to record the existence of abstracting and indexing services for an item.

Statements of volumes and/or dates covered by cumulative indexes of an item and a statement of location of these indexes. Indexes may be issued as part of an issue of the serial or issued separately.

CONSER Editing Guide, 1994 ed.:
Field 555 contains a statement of volumes and/or dates covered by cumulative indexes for a serial and a statement of location of these indexes, whether issued as part of the serial or issued separately. Input different types of indexes and different types of index notes (i.e., formal vs. informal) in separate 555 fields.

Do not confuse field 555 with field 510, which is used to record abstracting and indexing services. A cumulative index is indicated in a 555 note when it is an integral part of the serial. Field 510 is used when the indexing is external to the publication in hand.

✦ Editors' note: For indexes published separately, see "580 Linking Entry Complexity Note."

✦ Editors' note: The notes in this section are listed as they would appear on the catalog card, with the exception that the print constant "Indexes:" which would normally begin each note has been omitted. For instructions on tagging the 555 field, see the OCLC *Bibliographic Formats and Standards* and the *CONSER Editing Guide*.

FORMAL NOTES

1. Vols. 1 (1961)-4 (1966) in v. 4 of: Columbia journal of transnational law.
2. Vol. 2, no. 2 (1968)-v. 5, no. 1 (spring 1970) in the Journal of international law and economics, v. 9, no. 3 (1974).
3. Vols. 1-20, 1843/49-1899 (Issued as v. 21, pt. 1) 1 v.; Vols. 21-40, 1900-20, in v. 44; Vols. 21-60, 1900-40 (Issued as American Oriental series, v. 40) 1 v.
4. Vols. 1-11, 1967-78, with v. 11 (includes index to earlier title); v. 1-25, 1967-92 (includes index to earlier title). 1 v.
5. Vols. 2 (1926)-10 (1935) in v. 10 of later title.
6. Vols. 1 (1959)-10 (1968) (Includes index to journal under its earlier and later titles).
7. 1912-1957. 1 v. (Includes index to journal under its earlier and later titles.)
8. Author indexes: issues 1 (1966)-12 (1970). 1 v.; issues 13 (1971)-24 (1974). 1 v.; issues 25 (1975)-36 (1979). 1 v.; issues 37 (1980)-48 (1985/1986). 1 v.; issues 49 (1987)-60 (1992). 1 v.
9. Author Index: Vol. 1 (1976)- with v. 2- ; subject index: Vol. 1 (1976)- with v. 2-
10. New ser. Vols. 1 (1940)-6 (1946). 1 v.

INFORMAL NOTES

1. Includes decennial indexes.
2. Annual index in some issues.
3. Annual author and subject indexes.
4. Complete title, subject, and author index published on a 5-issue and 10-issue basis.
5. Subject indexes, cumulative from 1964, included in vols. for 1965-
6. Each vol. includes cumulative index to preceding vols.
7. The last vol. for each session is (or includes) a general index for the vols. in that session.
8. Index of contents, v. 1 (1961)-16 (1974) published separately in 1975.
9. Index published separately each year.
10. Each issue contains cumulative index to all issues.
11. Index to ASTM standards issued as last part of each vol.

12. Cumulative indexes published semiannually, 1975-1979,
    -1994; 1980-198 , <1996-> one semiannual index issued
    for Jan.-June.

13. Vol. 53, no. 4 constitutes cumulative index to Inland bird
    banding and the titles which preceded it.

14. With the 1979 edition a cumulated index covering the
    documents lists 1975-1979 has been produced.

15. Index for FY 73-FY 80, published in 1 vol., also covers serial
    under its earlier title: Federal program evaluations.

16. Each USAPat disc set contains a cumulative index that
    includes all patents on all discs published to date. Use any
    disc to run the INSTALL program in order to access the most
    recent cumulative index.

INFORMATION ABOUT DOCUMENTATION NOTE

DEFINITION/SCOPE

OCLC Bibliographic Formats and Standards, 2nd ed.:
Note about the documentation of the file, including code books and other accompanying material, that explain the content and use of the file.

If the note is about the use, study or analysis of the file, use field 581.

CONSER Editing Guide, 1994 ed.:
Use field 556 to record information about the documentation of computer file serials that explains their contents and use. Documentation may be published in print accompanying the computer file, or may be available by remote access.

Accompanying material other than the documentation for the file can be described in a 500 general note.

1. Accompanied by users' guide.
2. Accompanied by user's manual and quick reference guide.
3. Accompanied by user's guide issued <-May 1994> with title: APSRS CD-ROM users manual; issued <Aug. 1994>-199 with title: APSRS CD-ROM documentation.
4. Contains full-text user's manual on disc.
5. Accompanying manual: Artikelbasen på CD-ROM, Dokumentation (73 p. ; 30 cm.).
6. Accompanied by a user's guide in both English and French.
7. Accompanied by supplementary print resource called: Electronic clipper options : how to tips & techniques.
8. Accompanied by user manual and domain manual.

PROVENANCE NOTE

DEFINITION/SCOPE

OCLC Bibliographic Formats and Standards, 2nd ed.:
Notes about the history of the materials from the time of their creation to the time of their accession, including the date at which individual items or groups of items were first brought together in their current arrangement or collation.

Use field 561 for original or historical graphic material, three-dimensional artifacts, and naturally occurring objects.

If the note is about the immediate source of acquisition, use field 541.

Because this note is not generally used in serial records, it is not defined in *CONSER Editing Guide*, 1994 ed.

COPY AND VERSION IDENTIFICATION NOTE

DEFINITION/SCOPE

OCLC Bibliographic Formats and Standards, 2nd ed.:
Note that distinguishes the copies or versions of materials if more than one copy or version exists or could exist.

If the note is about a manuscript existing in two or more versions in single or multiple copies, use field 250.

If the note is about a reproduction, use field 533.

Because this note is not generally used in serial records, it is not defined in *CONSER Editing Guide*, 1994 ed.

CASE FILE CHARACTERISTICS NOTE

DEFINITION/SCOPE

OCLC Bibliographic Formats and Standards, 2nd ed.:
Notes about the content and characteristics of case files. Case files are records with standard categories of information about a defined population. Case files may be individual documents that have information about a single unit of analysis. They may reflect aggregate data (e.g., machine-readable records) that can be subdivided into individual case documents.

For computer files. Use field 565 for the number of cases or variables making up the file. This information, in conjunction with the number of logical records recorded in field 256, provides an indication of the extent of the file.

Because this note is not generally used in serial records, it is not defined in *CONSER Editing Guide*, 1994 ed.

METHODOLOGY NOTE

DEFINITION/SCOPE

OCLC Bibliographic Formats and Standards, 2nd ed.:
Notes for the significant methodological characteristics of the item (e.g., algorithm, universe description, sampling procedures, classi-fication, or validation characteristics).

Because this note is not generally used in serial records, it is not defined in *CONSER Editing Guide*, 1994 ed.

570

EDITOR NOTE (OBSOLETE)

LINKING ENTRY
COMPLEXITY NOTE

♦ Editors' note: The following text draws heavily on sections that cover the 580 note field and the 765-787 linking entry fields in the *OCLC Bibliographic Formats and Standards,* 2nd ed., the *CONSER Editing Guide,* 1994 ed., and the *CONSER Cataloging Manual.* This general purpose work has omitted examples for two relationships: 1) the Main series/Subseries pair (760/762), because they are input only by ISSN centers, and 2) the Host item (773), because it is used primarily in monographic records that are "in" analytics. The 773 is used for serials only when Leader/07 is set to value "b" (for serial component part). It is defined in OCLC as a printing field with a display constant (*In:*). (At the time of this writing, notes about this "Host item" relationship are not expressed in CONSER records.) As with other linking entry fields, if the display constant and linking entry title cannot adequately define the relationship, use a 580 note to describe it.

DEFINITION/SCOPE

Field 580 is used to express notes about complex relationships that cannot accurately be generated by using the display constants associated with the linking entry fields (765-787). It is also used for regular-print reprints to provide details of the original. (For relationships involving the 776 field (Additional physical form entry), see the section on note 530, "Additional Physical Form Available Note.")

If you use field 580, you must also use the appropriate defined linking fields for the related publication unless that publication cannot be named. In contrast, the 765-787 fields can be used without an accompanying 580 field whenever the display constant associated with the field adequately defines the relationship between the publications. When the print constant for the linking field does not adequately define the relationship or when your automated system does not generate an adequate display from the linking field, input a note in field 580 and suppress display of the corresponding linking field to avoid redundancy in the public catalog.

(Editors' note: For records contributed to a shared bibliographic utility, consult the utility's documentation for guidance on print constants and on the use of indicators in the linking field to control display of that field. For local input, consult your automated system documentation for similar guidance.)

You may create 580 notes to describe the following types of complex relationships between the title being cataloged and a related publication:

Original language (765)

Translation (767)

Supplement/special issue (770)

Parent record (772)

Other edition available (775)

Issued with (777)

Preceding title (780)

Succeeding title (785)

Nonspecific relationship (787)

Specifically, field 580 is used in the following situations:

1. When optional date information is provided with a "continued by" or "absorbed by" note. (Editors' note: The *CONSER Editing Guide* requires a 580 note in this circumstance; *OCLC Bibliographic Formats and Standards* does not. The present work includes examples with the optional date information. Follow the appropriate guidelines when contributing records to a shared utility. In addition, consult your local system documentation to ensure adequate local OPAC displays.)

2. When more than one entry is mentioned in a specific linking entry relationship note, such as "Split into: and: ," or "Merged with: to form: ". (Editors' note: The *CONSER Editing Guide* requires a 580 note in this circumstance; in contrast, *OCLC Bibliographic Formats and Standards* requires a 580 note only when three or more titles are involved. The present work includes examples for splits or mergers involving either two titles only or three or more titles. You should follow the appropriate guidelines when contributing records to a shared utility. In addition, consult your own system documentation to achieve adequate displays in the local OPAC.)

3. When the relationship cannot be expressed by a display constant in the linking entry field.

4. For notes pertaining to a regular-print reprint to provide details of the original publication.

5. When the serial bears a relationship to a monograph or other non-serial format publication, this relationship can be expressed in a 580 note when no linking field is given. (Linking fields can be given for monographs or other types of materials, but this is a matter of institutional policy. At the time of this writing, CONSER institutions have chosen not to link to monographs.)

6. When the serial bears a relationship to one or more publications that cannot be named, explain the relationship in a 580 note and do not provide any linking entry field.

7. When a serial is issued in more than one frequency and two or more records are required, relate one frequency edition to another using a 580 note.

8. When the physical format in which the serial is issued changes.

✦ Editors' note: The arrangement of the present section on field 580 encourages the cataloger first to determine the nature of the relationship and whether it calls for a linking entry field (767-787), then to decide what sort of note, if any, is called for. For guidance in this process, consult 1) the sections on field 580 in the most current editions of the *OCLC Bibliographic Formats and Standards* and the *CONSER Editing Guide* and 2) Module 14 ("Linking Relationships") of the most current edition of the *CONSER Cataloging Manual*.

ORIGINAL LANGUAGE

(Corresponding linking entry field: 765.)

1. Translation of: Problemy Dal'nego Vostoka, published by the Far East Institute, USSR Academy of Sciences.
2. Translation of its Cofiec informe anual.
3. Includes Italian translations of articles originally published in: Biologie médicale (SPECIA (Society)).
4. "Abridged translation of Mashinovedenie".
5. "English digest of the Soviet bimonthly, Mashinovedeniye".

TRANSLATION

(Corresponding linking entry field: 767.)

1. Cover to cover translation published as: Soviet machine science, 1983-1989.

2. Abridged translation published as: Mechanical sciences - Mashinovedenie, 1972-1982.

SUPPLEMENT/SPECIAL ISSUE

(Corresponding linking entry field: 770; for supplements not published separately or not input as a separate record, see "525 Supplement Note.")

1. Has supplement, 1974-1992 called: Corporate action; 1993- , called: Directory of corporate affiliations. Supplement.
2. La Chronique des arts et de la curiosité issued as a supplement, 1861-1922.
3. Has supplements: Program of the meeting - Acoustical Society of America, ISSN 0163-0962, and: References to contemporary papers on acoustics, ISSN 0163-0970 (published bimonthly prior to 1975 in regular issues).
4. Vols. for 1982- have supplement: Standard & Poor's international creditweek; Sept. 1985- have also supplement: Standard & Poor's creditreview; 1986- have also supplement: Creditweek international ratings guide.
5. Vols. for 1982- have numerous supplements covering various geographic world areas: Western Europe, Eastern Europe, USSR, Asia, South Asia, China, Middle East and North Africa, Sub-Saharan Africa, Western Hemisphere, North America and Oceania, Latin America, etc. Supplements for 1982 have common title: Review of agriculture in . . . and outlook for . . .; supplements for 1983- have common title: World agriculture regional supplement . . .
6. Supplemented by print publication with accompanying diskette entitled: Stata technical bulletin.
7. Supplemented by: National income and product accounts of the United States. Statistical tables, 1965- ; by: Business statistics (Washington, D.C. : Biennial), 1951- ; by: Weekly business statistics, 1977-1981, and by their predecessor and successor publications.
8. Issues for 1983- supplemented by: Medical subject headings. Supplementary chemical records.
9. Kept up-to-date by periodic supplements: Merchant marine examination questions. New & revised engineering questions.
    ✦ [Editors' note: For additional 580 notes describing updating supplements, see "Updates" in the subsection "Nonspecific Relationships."]

10. Beginning Sept. 28, 1960 each issue accompanied by: Science teacher's world.
11. Issues for July 1952-1964 accompanied by: Statistical supplement, formerly included in statistics section of the Review, and was superseded in 1965 by: Bulletin of labour statistics.
    ◆ [AACR2R: . . . and was continued in 1965 . . .]
12. Some issues for 1976-85 accompanied by supplement with title: Recent literature; for 1986- with title: Recent ornithological literature.
    ◆ [AACR2R: 1976-1985]
13. Vols. for 1960/61-1979/80 have special issue: Assistantships and fellowships in mathematics; v. for 1980/81-1988/89 have special issue: Assistantships and fellowships in the mathematical sciences.
14. Includes a special number published in the summer of 1971 called "The Intrepid-Bear issue: Intrepid 20/Floating Bear 38."
15. Includes: Datapro small computers news.
16. In 1977, the publishers of Back stage took over the publication of Business screen, calling it a supplement to Back stage; in 1978-1979, the title was changed to Business and home TV screen, and continued as a supplement to Back stage; in 1979-1980, the title became Back stage magazine supplement/ Business screen, and was issued as a monthly supplement called "section two" of Back stage; from 1980-1982, the title reverted to Business screen, and was still called "section two, monthly supplement" to Back stage.

PARENT RECORD

(Corresponding linking entry field: 772.)

1. Vol. 1 published as a special issue of: The Jurist.
2. Annual June special issue of: Euromoney.
3. Issued every July as the "Directory issue" of: Public relations journal.
4. Issued as an annual supplement to: Nature.
5. Issued as section 2 magazine supplement of: Back stage.
6. Issued as suppl. to: Industrie minérale, 1980- ; to: Industrie minérale, mines et carrières, 1985- ; to: Mines & carrières, 1988-
7. Vols. 1-3 issued as a supplement to Brain research; v. 4- to Neuroscience.

8. Vols. for 1981/82- issued as supplement two to: The book of the States.
9. Vols. 1 (1940)-3 (1943) issued as supplement to the: Gemmologist.
10. Vols. for 1976-1982 issued as supplement to: Auk; 1983- as supplement to: Auk, and: Ibis.
11. Supplement to, or in some years an issue of: Instrument manufacturing.
12. A periodic supplement to: The Directory of directories.
13. Special supplement to: Euromoney, and: Global investor.
14. English suppl. to the Journal of the Cerrahpadşa Medical Faculty.
15. Electronic supplement to: Annals of improbable research.
16. Supplements the semiannual CD-ROM publication: Pressdok ; Hundok.
17. Updates, with Corporate updates: Taft corporate directory, 1982-1984; Taft corporate giving directory, 1985-
    ✦ [Editors' note: For additional 580 notes describing updating supplements, see "Updates" in the section on "Nonspecific Relationships."]
18. Serves as advance sheets for: Ohio State reports, 3rd ser.; Ohio appellate reports, 3rd ser.; and Ohio miscellaneous reports, 2nd ser.
19. Each issue contains additions or changes to questions in some or all sections of: Merchant marine examination questions.
20. Statistics for 1949-1954 published in Sept. issues of: Social security bulletin (Washington, D.C. : 1938), 1950-1955.
21. A pullout section of: Advertising age.
22. Summary of the monthly publication: Direction of trade statistics.
    ✦ [Option: Consider the title in question to be a summary rather than a supplement; substitute linking entry field 787 for 772.]

OTHER EDITION AVAILABLE

(Corresponding linking entry field: 775.)

A. General
   1. Issued also in a college edition, 1928-39.
      ✦ [AACR2R: 1928-1939]
   2. Issued 1842-1901 also in an American edition (called: London lancet, 1842-1892; Lancet, 1895-1897; New York lancet, 1898-1901) and in a North American edition, July 1966-

3. Issued outside Australia as Journey, <1983>-1989.
4. Outside of North and South America, published as: Information trade directory, ISSN 0142-0208.
5. Pub. also in Norfolk, Conn. by New Directions.
   ◆ [AACR2R: Published also . . .]
6. Expanded companion edition of: Information Moscow.
   ◆ [Option: Consider Information Moscow to be a companion publication; substitute linking entry field 787 for 775.]

B. Other language editions
   1. Issued also in an English ed., 1955-1966.
   2. Issued also in Russian and v. 2- in English.
   3. Published also in German and Spanish editions.
   4. Also published in English ed. with same title.
   5. Also published in French under title: Sommaire des Communications, ISSN 0226-7489.
   6. Also published in Chinese: Kuang kao tsa chih.
   7. Issued also in an Italian-language ed. (with different textual content), published: Milano : Esquire, 1990-
   8. Also issued in French, Spanish and Portuguese editions, 1968- ; in a German edition, 1970- ; in an Arabic edition, 1980- ; and in a Chinese edition, 1983-

C. Reprint editions
   1. Reprint. Originally published quarterly: New York, N.Y. : The Armchair Detective, Inc.
   2. Reprint, with an introduction. Originally published biweekly (irregular): Lima : [s.n.].
   3. Reprint with an introduction. Originally published monthly: México : Escuela Normal Primaria para Maestros.
   4. Reprint, with an introduction, of a monthly periodical published in Mexico.
   5. Reprint, with two supplements added: Dav a censúra, and Bibliografia "Davu". Originally published irregularly: Praha : íL. Obtulovič, 1924-1925; Bratislava : Zd. Merc (varies), 1926-1937.
   6. Reprint, with an introduction. Originally published in Mexico : [s.n.].
   7. Reprint, with an introduction added, of a periodical published in Cambridge, Mass., Bronx, New York, and San Francisco.

8. Reprint, with introduction and new material added, of a newsletter published in New York and edited by D. Di Prima, 1961-69 (with L. Jones, 1961-62).
  ✦ [AACR2R: 1961-1969 . . . 1961-1962]
9. Reprint of a periodical published in Paris and New York.
10. Reprint of the publication with same title.
11. Reprint. Originally published under title: Kengaku kiroku, Feb. 1939-Jan. 1940; continued by: Owari no iseki to ibutsu, Feb. 1940-July 1944. Monthly, Feb. 1939-Dec, 1942; irregular, Feb. 1942-July 1944: Nagoya-shi : Nagoya Kyōdo Kenkyukai.
12. Reprint, with an introduction, of a periodical published 1928-<1935>
13. Reprint of the Aug. issue of Art in America.

ISSUED WITH

(Corresponding linking entry field: 777.)

A. Issued with
  1. Issued in: Childhood education, Sept./Oct. 1981-Nov./Dec. 1981.
  2. Issued with and included in subscription to: Legal times.
  3. Published with: Euromoney.
  4. One no. a year issued jointly with: Yiddish, ISSN 0364-4308, and called, 1977: Conference on Modern Jewish Studies annual, ISSN 0270-9392; called 1978-<79>: Modern Jewish studies annual, ISSN 0270-9406.
    ✦ [AACR2R: 1978-<1979>]
  5. Issued annually as an unnumbered 4th issue of: Housing and society.
  6. Vols. for 1956-1968 issued as the Sept. number of the Journal of Asian studies.
  7. Vols. for 1981- issued with: Wall street journal. Index (New York, N.Y.).
  8. Issues for Oct. 1950-Dec. 1950 and <Jan. 1957-> issued with: Transactions of the Institution of Mining and Metallurgy; Jan. 1951-<Nov. 1955> include only the transactions' title page and the contents page, the transactions published separately; -Dec. 1975 issued with Sections A, B, and C of the transactions.
  9. Issued Nov. 1873-Dec. 1895 under same cover with: American Society of Civil Engineers. Transactions of the American Society of Civil Engineers.

10. Some v. for -1977/78 issued as part of the serial: Gallup opinion index; for <1982-1987> issued as part of the serial: Gallup report (Princeton, N.J. : 1981).
11. An annual publication called: Religion in America was issued in some years during <1982-1987> in lieu of a regular monthly issue.
12. Issued 1995-1996 with every second issue of: Angewandte Chemie, ISSN 0570-0833; and: Angewandte Chemie (Weinheim an der Bergstrasse, Germany), ISSN 0044-8249; issued separately, 1997-
13. Vol. 33, no. 2- issued with: Voice of Chorus America.
14. Issue for spring 1982 is a special section of: Landscape architecture.
15. Vol. for 1960 is a reprint of no. 1-6, Feb.-Dec. 1960 which were issued jointly with: Communications of the ACM.

B. "Includes" statements (For examples of titles not published separately, see "500 General Note.")
    1. Includes issues for -Dec. 1975 of: Bulletin (Institution of Mining and Metallurgy (Great Britain)).
    2. Includes a separately numbered title: Monthly statement.
    3. Includes: National formulary, 15th ed.-
    4. Includes "Elenchus bibliographicus biblicus", v. 1-48, 1920-67 (published independently, 1968-).
        ✦ [AACR2R: 1920-1967]
    5. Vol. 1-4; 1967-1971, includes v. 12-16 of Metallurgical reviews.
    6. Vols. for 1956-1968 include Bibliography of Asian studies as the Sept. issue. Beginning with 1969 this bibliography is issued separately.
    7. Vols. 1-23/24 (1891/92-1913/14) include: Annales de géographie. Bibliographie, 1891-1898; Bibliographie géographique annuelle, 1899-1914.
    8. Vols. for <1980-> include semi-annually: Designers west resource directory.
    9. Vols. for 1971- include also: Annual report of the Division of Land Reclamation.
    10. Vols. for <1982-> include the Harris Ohio buyers industrial directory, also issued separately.
    11. Vols. for 1958-<66> include alternate biennial revisions of: Current drug handbook, ISSN 0070-1939, also issued separately.
        ✦ [AACR2R: 1962-<1966>]

12. Alternate biennial revisions for 1962/64-<1966/68> also included in: The Drug, the nurse, the patient.
13. Occasional issues for 1964- include 2nd- International directory of anthropological institutions.
14. Issues for fall 1991- alternately include separately paged issues of American choral review, v. 33, no. 2- ; and the Research memorandum series (American Choral Foundation), both previously published separately.
15. Issues for Sept. 1966-May/June 1981 include: ACEI branch exchange; issues for Sept./Oct. 1981-Nov./Dec. 1981 include: ACEI exchange.

PRECEDING TITLE

(Corresponding linking entry field: 780.)

A. Continuations
   1. Called new series in 1980, in continuation of: Acta embryologiae experimentalis.
   2. Continues a bimonthly publication with the same title issued 19 -1966.
   3. With similar titles, continues: Proceedings (American Society of Civil Engineers), ISSN 0097-417X.
   4. With: National accounts statistics. Analysis of main aggregates, and: National accounts statistics. Government accounts and tables, continues: United Nations. Statistical Office. Yearbook of national accounts statistics.
   5. Supersedes the separate language editions: Assignment children (Neuilly-sur-Seine, France) and: Carnets de l'enfance (Neuilly-sur-Seine, France), and: Kinder dieser Welt.
      ✦ [AACR2R: Continues the separate language editions . . .]
   6. Continues v. 3 of: United States. Energy Information Administration. Annual report to Congress.
   7. Continues pt. 1 of Aug. issue of: Hospitals (Chicago, Ill. : 1936), called "guide issue," 1956-1970.
   8. Continues the index section of: Current abstracts of chemistry and index chemicus.
   9. Continues the monthly issues, Jan.-Nov., of: Balance of payments yearbook.
   10. Formerly published as part of: Martindale-Hubbell law directory.
   11. Formerly issued as a section of: Directory: home centers & hardware chains, auto supply chains.

12. Issued previously as a supplement to Die Technik.
13. Previously published as a separately paginated section in: Water & sewage works.
14. No. 1-11 appeared as a section of: Kurtrierisches Jahrbuch, 1969-1979.
    ✦ [Option: Consider the title to have been issued with Kurtrierisches Jahrbuch and substitute linking field 777 for 780.]
15. Formerly International law digests volumes of: Martindale-Hubbell law digest.
16. Prior to Aug. 1977, the newsletter was published as alternate issues of the NARD journal.
17. Earlier v. issued as part of: City finances.
18. Information formerly included in: Annual energy outlook.
19. First report issued as 1987, no. 3 of: Brookings papers on economic activity.

B. Continuations in different formats
    1. Continues a tabloid publication with the same title.
    2. Continues the print version with the same title.
    3. Continues the print serial: Monash University. Research report - Monash University.
    4. Continues the print format: Lighthouse (University Park, Pa.).
    5. Continues print title: Value line industry review.
    6. Continues a periodical with the same name issued in paper format.

C. Mergers or unions
    1. Merger of: New scientist; and: Science journal, and continues the numbering of the former.
    2. Merger of: ECS; and in part: Proceedings of the Institution of Electrical Engineers.
        ✦ [Better: Merger of: ECS; and the "Electronics" section of Proceedings of the Institution of Electrical Engineers.]
    3. Formed by the merger of: Current mortality analysis; Monthly marriage report; and: Monthly vital statistics bulletin.
    4. Formed by the union of: Acta geobotanica Barcinonensia, and: Acta phytotaxonomica Barcinonensia, and assumes numbering of the sum of their issues.
    5. Formed by the union of: Dansk artikelindeks, and by: Dansk artikelindeks (Monthly).

D. Absorptions
   1. With v. 22, no. 1, Jan. 1987, absorbed: Subject guide to forthcoming books.
   2. Absorbed: Association for Childhood Education International. ACEI exchange with fall 1991 issue.
   3. Beginning with new ser. v. 12 (July 1952) incorporates the Bibliography of industrial diamond applications which continues its own vol. numbering, v. 9, etc.
   4. Vols. for 1957-1963 include section: "Washington municipal news," previously issued as a separate publication.
   5. Occasional issues, June 15, 1981- include: ESF synchrotron radiation news, no. 6- , issued by European Science Foundation, continuing: European synchrotron radiation news.
      ✦ [Editors' note: ESF synchrotron radiation news occurs in a 777 linking entry field, European synchrotron radiation news in a 780 field.]

SUCCEEDING TITLE

(Corresponding linking entry field: 785.)

A. Continuations
   1. Continued in 1983 by: Outlook and situation report. World agriculture.
   2. Continued in part by: Journal of geophysical research. Oceans; and: Journal of geophysical research. Atmospheres.
   3. Continued in part by an abstracts section called: Current abstracts of chemistry; and an index section called: Index chemicus (Philadelphia, Pa. : 1977).
   4. In 1987, when the sections separated, this publication was continued in part by: Musical America (New York, N.Y. : 1987), and by: High fidelity (Great Barrington, Mass. : 1959).
   5. Continued as a section within: Index medicus, ISSN 0019-3879, and: Cumulated index medicus, ISSN 0090-1423.
   6. "Letters to the Editor" section continued by: Journal of materials science letters.
   7. Product directory section continued by: ASHRAE product specification file, which accompanies each volume of ASHRAE handbook.
   8. Pt. 1 of Aug. issue continued in 1971 by: Hospital statistics (American Hospital Association); pt. 2 of August issue continued in 1972 by: AHA guide to the health care field.

9. Alternate issues for Sept. 1970-July 1977 published in "newsletter format," continued separately Aug. 1977- as: National Association of Retail Druggists (U.S.). NARD newsletter.
10. Includes unnumbered section called Library marketplace, which continues as independent publication.
    ◆ [Better: Includes unnumbered section called Library marketplace, which continues as independent publication, Nov. 1974-]
11. Issues for 1946- contain unnumbered supplement: Schweisstechnik, later issued separately.
12. Information on energy data (v. 2) and projections (v. 3) issued separately, 1982- in: Annual energy review, and: Annual energy outlook.
13. Assessment of international energy markets, 1985- published separately as: International energy outlook.
14. Included: Industrial wastes (Chicago, Ill. : 1971), separately numbered, now published separately.

B. Continuations in different formats
    1. Continued in 1994 as: Index translationum (CD-ROM).
    2. Continued on diskette as: Research, scholarship, creative and performing art (Windows version). Monash University.
    3. Continued in 1996 only on diskette as: Energy statistics handbook (Diskette).
    4. Continued in diskette format by: Industry review.

C. Mergers
    1. Merged with: IEE proceedings. I, Solid-state and electron devices, to form: IEE proceedings. G, Circuits, devices and systems.
    2. Merged with: Mexico update, to form the monthly publication: Business Mexico (Mexico City, Mexico : 1991).
    3. Merged with: Part B (Organic chemistry) of Chemische Berichte, ISSN 0009-2940, to form: Liebigs Annalen.
    4. Merged with its monthly ed.: Dansk artikelindeks (Monthly), to form: Artikelbasen.
    5. Merged with: Indiagram. Week's news, and: India economic newsletter, to form: India news (Washington, D.C. : 1962), issued Apr. 27, 1962- with new volume numbering.

D. Absorptions
1. Absorbed by: Childhood education, beginning with Oct. 1991.
2. Absorbed by: Scott stamp monthly, as a separately numbered section Nov. 1983.
3. Issued 1964- as a section of: Nation's cities (continuing its own vol. numbering).
4. Reports for 1957-75 included in Jan. issues of its: Business review (Federal Reserve Bank of Philadelphia).
    ✦ [AACR2R: 1957-1975]

E. Splits
1. Split into: Balance of payments statistics, and: Balance of payments statistics. Yearbook.
2. Split into: ASHRAE handbook. Fundamentals; ASHRAE handbook. Applications; ASHRAE handbook. Equipment, and: ASHRAE handbook. Systems.
3. Split into several subseries under the common title: Garcia de Orta.
4. In Jan. 1984 split into: Comptes rendus de l'Académie des sciences. Vie des sciences, and: Académie des sciences (France). Nouvelles de l'Académie.
5. Superseded by the separate language editions: Carnets de l'enfance (Geneva, Switzerland) and: Assignment children (Geneva, Switzerland).
    ✦ [AACR2R: Continued by the separate language editions . . .]

NONSPECIFIC RELATIONSHIP

(Corresponding linking entry field: 787.)

A. Shared contents
1. Includes data from the current Social indicators of development, World debt tables, World tables, and Trends in developing economies, each issued also in print.
2. Records include publications from: Bibliography on cold regions science and technology; and Antarctic bibliography.
3. Includes information found in: Million dollar directory; and: Reference book of corporate managements.
4. Includes: Forestry abstracts, 1939- ; Forest products abstracts, 1978- ; and Agroforestry abstracts, 1988-

5. Contains citations from: Bowker's complete video directory, and full-text reviews from: Variety (New York, N.Y.).
6. Consists of three files corresponding to: Vol. 1 of Encyclopedia of associations; Encyclopedia of associations. International organizations; and: Encyclopedia of associations. Regional, state, and local organizations.
7. Also available as part of CD-ROM: SciTech reference plus.
8. Science/technology-oriented parts also available as part of CD-ROM: SciTech reference plus.
9. Also issued as part of: Staff directories on CD-ROM, <1993->
10. Some tables also available on CD-ROM: Vital Registration System annual statistical files, births and deaths.

B. Previous publication
   1. Includes information previously presented in: Weekly coal production, ISSN 0733-0545 and in: Coal distribution, ISSN 0737-4399.
   2. Comprises, in tabular form, all of the information previously published in: Bulletin of the International Seismological Centre.
   3. The series published in the Bulletin also appear in the Year book of labour statistics.
   4. Expanded and edited papers selected from: Ti ch^{c}iu hua hsüeh.
   5. Some material appearing in Survey of current business is occasionally reprinted in the publication: User's guide to BEA information.
   6. Softcover reissue of the subject index portion of: Engineering index annual.
      ✦ [Option: Consider this publication to be an edition; substitute linking entry field 775 for 787.]
   7. Beginning with 1987, the physical vols. comprising the subject index are reissued in a separate softcover edition with title: Engineering index subject index.
      ✦ [Option: Consider this publication to be an edition; substitute linking entry field 775 for 787.]
      ✦ [Option for examples 8-14: Consider these to be reprints; substitute linking entry field 775 for 787.]
   8. Vol. 1 is a reissue of: Etudes géographiques, 1re année, fasc. 1 (janv. 1900)-1re année, fasc. 4 (oct. 1900).
   9. Contents reprinted from: AIA journal.
   10. Contains collected reprints of articles from: Parasitology.

11. Compilations of articles reprinted from: Gulf-Coast Association of Geological Societies. Transactions - Gulf Coast Association of Geological Societies.
12. Selected articles are reprinted in: Readings in Gulf Coast geology.
13. A collection of contributions to: The American mercury (New York, N.Y. : 1924).
14. Most no. are reprints from or supplements to Circulation, Circulation research, or Hypertension.

C. Issued as

♦ Editors' note: Common cataloging practice provides the alternative of using the 777 linking entry field when the related title either is published separately at some time during its run or has a numbering scheme separate from the title it is issued with. Although the related titles in the following examples are tagged 787, you may consider using 777 in these or similar circumstances when one or the other of the above stipulations is met. For additional examples, see subsection "Issued with."

1. Issues for 1979- issued as special Nursing job guide issue of Nursing job news and dated Jan. 15.
2. Vol. 2 of the Annual report issued separately as: Merger decisions.
   ♦ [Better: Vol. 2 of the Annual report issued separately 1981-19   as: Merger decisions.]
3. Some volumes issued as Part 2 of one number of the Bulletin of the American Mathematical Society.
4. Issued as a section of: Journal of molecular structure, and included in its numbering also.
5. Some nos. also published separately as: Documentary edition of American perfumer & aromatics.
6. Some volumes have also title: Theochem, which, until 1995, also had its own numbering.
7. Executive summary, foreword, introduction, categories of chemicals catalogued, and the Regulatory Council's statement on setting priorities for regulating carcinogens, for 1980 also issued separately as: Annual report on carcinogens. Executive summary.

D. Cumulations, compilations, summaries
1. Cumulated by: Deutsche Bibliographie. Halbjahres-Verzeichnis, and by: Deutsche Bibliographie. Fünfjahres-Verzeichnis.

2. Cumulated by: Bibliography of agriculture. Annual cumulation, 1980-1982; and: Bibliography of agriculture. Annual cumulative indexes.
    ✦ [Better: . . . Annual cumulative indexes, 1983-]
3. Cumulated annually by: F&S index Europe annual (Foster City, Calif.).
4. Cumulated 1994- by annual CD-ROM publication of the same title.
    ✦ [Option: Consider the difference in physical format more important to bring out than the cumulating function; substitute note field 530 for 580 and linking entry field 776 for 787.]
5. Data were cumulated quinquennially in Surface water supply of the United States.
6. Groups of ten issues cumulated in: Advance data from Vital and health statistics.
7. Cumulates listings in quarterly paper issues of the same title.
8. Cumulates monthly paper publication of the same title.
    ✦ [Option: Consider the difference in physical format more important to bring out than the cumulating function; substitute note field 530 for 580 and linking entry field 776 for 787.]
9. Cumulates: Deutsche Bibliographie. Wöchentliches Verzeichnis, 1953-1964, and its several successor parts, 1965-1990.
10. Cumulation of the monthly publication: F&S index United States.
11. Cumulation of the quarterly publication with same title.
12. Annual cumulation of a bimonthly publication with the same title.
13. Issued also in an annual cumulation with title: Cumulated index medicus, ISSN 0090-1423.
14. Vols. for 1968- are cumulations of: Engineering index monthly; 1971- of: Engineering index monthly and author index; 1984- of: Engineering index monthly (New York, N.Y. : 1984).
15. Quinquennial cumulations issued as vols. of the quinquennial cumulations of: National union catalog, ISSN 0028-0348.
16. Compilation of the monthly publication: Insider newsletter.
17. Issues for 1980-1981 compiled into: Annual insider; for 1982- into: Annual insider index to public policy studies.
18. "A digest of federal tax articles appearing in the Journal of taxation, Taxation for accountants, Taxation for lawyers."

19. Quarterly summaries of the data and other information significant to the area are published in: Labor market bulletin.
20. Combines all non-duplicative elements of: Overseas business reports.
21. A cumulation of the citations which appeared during 1977-78 in: Biogenic amines and transmitters in the nervous system, ISSN 0006-3077.

E. Updates (For updates that are supplements and that are not cataloged separately, see "525 Supplement Note"; for unnamed updates, see "500 General Note.")

◆ Editors' note: Common cataloging practice provides the alternative of using the 770 (supplement/special issue) or 772 (parent record) linking entry field rather than the 787 (nonspecific relationship) field when the 580 describes the relationship between a title and its updating supplement. Although the related titles in the following examples are tagged 787, you may consider using 770 or 772 even if the updating service does not call itself a supplement. For additional examples, see subsections "Supplement/Special Issue" and "Parent Record."

1. Kept up-to-date between editions by: America buys. Updating service.
2. Updated by: Law information update, a companion service issued ten times a year.
3. Kept updated by annual publication called Books in print supplement, 1972/73-   ; and bimonthly issues of Forthcoming books, 1966-
4. Updates information for: Books in print, and: Subject guide to Books in print.
5. A bi-monthly updating of: Books in print.

F. Indexes (For indexes not published separately, see "555 Cumulative Index/Finding Aid Note.")

1. Index to: Australian official journal of patents, trade marks, and designs.
2. Annual and cumulative index to: Government reports announcements & index, ISSN 0097-9007.
3. Indexes the microfiche collection: Curriculum development library.
4. Vols. 5- 1975- issued as the annual index to: Mathematical reviews, ISSN 0025-5629, v. 45-   1973-

5. Has an annual, cumulative index: Government reports annual index.
6. Related print index: Skorowidz przepisów prawnych ogłoszonych w Dzienniku ustaw I Monitorze polskim w latach . . .
7. Issues for <1982-> accompanied by printed publishers' index: Books in print microfiche publishers and distributors index; 1989- publishers' index included in microfiche.
8. Indexed by: Subject guide to books in print, 1957-1987/88; by: Books in print. Subject guide, 1988/89-
9. Vols. for 1957- issued as index to Publishers' trade list annual, ISSN 0079-7855.

G. Companion publications
   1. Companion to: Medical subject headings. Tree structures; Medical subject headings. Tree annotations; and to: Permuted medical subject headings.
   2. Companion series to the journal: Studies in language.
   3. Companion title to: CASSIS/CD-ROM.
   4. Companion publication to the image database of most of the indexed/abstracted titles: Magazine collection [microform]; and to the ASCII full text of most of the indexed/abstracted titles: Magazine ASAP [computer file].
   5. Companion vol. to: AHA guide to the health care field, 1972-1973; called: American Hospital Association guide to the health care field, 1974-
   6. Companion journals, 1990- : Journal of materials science. Materials in electronics; and: Journal of materials science. Materials in medicine.
   7. Issued as companion to: Journal of applied physics.
   8. Vols. for 1976- called v. 3, a companion volume to: Acronyms, initialisms, & abbreviations dictionary, ISSN 0270-4404.
   9. Has companion: Variety film reviews.
   10. Has annual companion publication: Anuario de arquitectura.
   11. Complemented by: Foundation directory. Part 2, a guide to grant programs, $25,000-$100,000.
   12. Vols. for 1990/91- complemented by: MLA directory of scholarly presses in language and literature. Modern Language Association of America.

13. Complemented by an annual listing of topical worldwide stamps as printed during the previous year in Scott stamp monthly, called: Scott . . . "by topic" stamp annual.
14. Complemented by: Statistical sources and methods, 1984-1992; and: Consumer price indices (Geneva, Switzerland), 1984-
15. Complemented by: Peterson's summer study abroad.
16. Discussion of assumptions underlying forecasts in the AEO in auxiliary publication: Assumptions for the annual energy outlook.

H. Miscellaneous nonspecific relationships

1. A joint issue of: Yiddish, ISSN 0364-4308, and: Studies in American Jewish literature, ISSN 0148-7663.
2. Based on auto reports appearing monthly in Consumer reports.
3. Short-term energy projections provided by: Short-term energy outlook.
4. Developed from a special report published annually, 1990- in a March issue of: U.S. news & world report; substantial excerpts continue to be published in a March issue of the magazine, <1994->
5. Selected papers from the 1st annual meeting included in: Journal of the Atlantic Provinces Linguistic Association, ISSN 0706-6910.
6. Assumes the vol. numbering of another publication with the same title, published in Halle since 1874.
7. Beginning in 1955 another edition is published in Tübingen with different editors and contents but which assumes the volume numbering of the Halle edition.
8. A competing version of this title with different content issued by Liverpool University Press, 1996-
9. Issued in competition with a version published 1996- with different content by University of Glasgow.
10. Combined distribution list for all reviews published in: Bryn Mawr classical review; and: BMMR (i.e., Bryn Mawr medieval review).
11. Also issued as v. 49, no. 1-2 of: Revue de l'Université d'Ottawa.
12. Published concurrently by the U.S. Bureau of Industrial Economics under the title: Franchise opportunities handbook.
    ✦ [Option: Consider this publication to be an edition; substitute linking entry field 775 for 787.]

13. Beginning with v. 10, no. 4, contents are the same as: Wage-price law and economics review, ISSN 0361-6665.
    ✦ [Option: Consider this publication to be an edition; substitute linking entry field 775 for 787.]

I. Related non-serial publications
    ✦ Editors' note: Some of the following examples are from records that include no linking entry field for the related non-serial publication. At the time of this writing, the use of the linking entry for non-serial publications is a matter of institutional policy.

    1. Separated from v. 2 of: Secured transactions in personal property in Canada by Richard H. McLaren, issued in loose-leaf format.
    2. Earlier information in: The Literature of American history, and its supplements.
    3. Continues monograph: Biographical directory of the United States Congress, 1774-1989.
    4. Continues the information in: Kokusai Bunka Shinkōkai. K.B.S. bibliography of standard reference books for Japanese studies, with descriptive notes.
    5. Based on the original print publication: Beilstein's Handbuch der organischen Chemie.
    6. Vol. 2 issued as supplement to the 2d edition of the ALA index to general literature.

PUBLICATIONS ABOUT DESCRIBED MATERIALS NOTE

DEFINITION/SCOPE

OCLC Bibliographic Formats and Standards, 2nd ed.:
Notes for the citation of, or information about, a publication based on the use, study, or analysis of the materials. Use field 581 for citations to published sources that contain photocopies or reproductions of items (e.g., exhibition or collection catalogs).

If the note is about the documentation of a computer file, use field 556.

Because this note is not generally used in serial records, it is not defined in *CONSER Editing Guide*, 1994 ed.

RELATED COMPUTER FILES NOTE (OBSOLETE)

DEFINITION/SCOPE

"This field was made obsolete because according to the guidelines agreed upon for separate notes its continued existence could not be justified. The information can be recorded in fields 787 (Nonspecific Relationship Entry) and 580 (Linking Entry Complexity Note)"—*Format Integration and Its Effect on the USMARC Bibliographic Format,* 1995 ed.

ACTION NOTE

DEFINITION/SCOPE

OCLC Bibliographic Formats and Standards, 2nd ed.:
Notes about processing and reference actions.

Because this note is not generally used in serial records, it is not
defined in *CONSER Editing Guide,* 1994 ed.

ACCUMULATION AND FREQUENCY OF USE NOTE

DEFINITION/SCOPE

OCLC Bibliographic Formats and Standards, 2nd ed.:
Notes about the accumulation of material and/or its frequency of use.

◆

Because this note is not generally used in serial records, it is not defined in *CONSER Editing Guide*, 1994 ed.

EXHIBITIONS NOTE

DEFINITION/SCOPE

OCLC Bibliographic Formats and Standards, 2nd ed.:
Notes about the exhibitions where the material has been shown.

Because this note is not generally used in serial records, it is not defined in *CONSER Editing Guide*, 1994 ed.

AWARDS NOTE

DEFINITION/SCOPE

OCLC Bibliographic Formats and Standards, 2nd ed.:
Notes about awards associated with the item.

Because this note is not generally used in serial records, it is not
defined in *CONSER Editing Guide*, 1994 ed.

SOURCES

The following section contains information that will be helpful in locating the bibliographic record from which a particular note was taken. The source information is arranged to correspond with the fields and subsections in the previous section.

The source entries include author (when present), title, Library of Congress Control Number (when present), and OCLC record number. For example:

(TITLE)	(LCCN)	(OCLC number)
1. Applied physics letters online	sn96-4285	#34787267

Please remember that the note that was present in the OCLC record at the time we used the record may have been revised or deleted.

246 VARYING FORM OF TITLE

SECOND INDICATOR Ƀ

1. Chicago morning herald (Chicago, Ill. : 1881)	sn82-6831	#8793212
2. U.S. government periodicals index (CD-ROM)	96-647244	#30081409
3. Human retroviruses and AIDS . . . compendium	sn96-47056	#35023343
4. NewsBank NewsFile	sn96-47045	#34564325
5. Applied physics letters online	sn96-4285	#34787267
6. Canadian General Standards Board CGSB's electronic catalogue ECAT	sn96-47040	#34848090
7. Notices of the American Mathematical Society (Online)	sn96-3966	#34550461
8. Court opinions reference disc	sn96-4298	#35163305
9. Opal United States immigration law library. Disc 1, Official forms	95-645695	#32210991
10. Journal of extension (Online)	sn94-2758	#28941991
11. Data report of oceanographic observations	sn96-47069	#35106961
12. Energy statistics handbook (Diskette)	sn96-32750	#35709875

13. Cornell political forum (Online)		#32877134
14. JAIR	sn95-35410	#32636311
15. TESS	sn96-47043	#34742135
16. AIDS book review journal	95-649661	#27670588
17. Bryn Mawr medieval review	sn93-6261	#28355218
18. BEN	sn96-15064	#31494053
19. Didaskalia (Hobart, Tas.)	sn96-23113	#32964472

SECOND INDICATOR 2

1. Commodity year book	39-11418	#2259600
2. Society for College and University Planning (Ann Arbor, Mich.). Selected Papers from the annual conference.	70-200014	#6880729

SECOND INDICATOR 3

1. Ammunition	46-18320	#5190717
2. Shakaigaku nenshi	73-819945	#1790081

SECOND INDICATOR 4

1. Library of Congress. Exchange and Gift Division. Monthly checklist of state publications	10-8924	#2553426
2. Qantas Empire Airways, ltd. Report and financial accounts for the fifteen months ended . . .	53-20101	#9400332
3. Annual report of statistics of criminal and other offences	73-641726	#1785421

SECOND INDICATOR 5

1. Canada. Agriculture Canada. Annual report of the minister under the Crop Insurance Act	81-645978	#7873077
2. Sudan guide	83-980355	#8755850

SECOND INDICATOR 6

1. Control systems magazine (New York, N.Y. : 1981)	81-649117	#8022749
2. Annual report (Reserve Bank of India. Central Board of Directors)	76-922405	#1799954

SECOND INDICATOR 7

1. Bangladesh Education Extension Centre bulletin	76-913473	#7505552
2. Association for the Care of Children in Hospitals. Journal of the Association for the Care of Children in Hospitals	77-644210	#2677212

SECOND INDICATOR 8

1. Acta biologica Hungarica	86-640505	#10705062
2. Knoxville College. Alumni directory	84-647168	#11205788

500 GENERAL NOTE

INFORMAL SCOPE NOTES

A. General contents information

1. American Society for Eighteenth Century Studies. ASECS directory	sn88-12909	#2430286
2. Media review	sn80-9192	#5934434
3. Nordicom. Bibliography of Nordic mass communications literature	79-646477	#4030466
4. Cahiers d'études et de recherches victoriennes et édouardiennes	sn82-21358	#4031084
5. Science resources studies highlights	sf83-1175	#3159753
6. Courtauld Institute illustration archives. Archive 2, 15th & 16th century sculpture in Italy	sn84-10383	#3998337
7. AMAA news	sc84-7471	#10411703
8. Statistical report (Alaska. Division of Social Services)	83-640059	#9099738
9. Environment (Dublin, Ohio)	sn90-3073	#18860308
10. InfoTrac	92-644672	#22288636
11. FEDSTAT	92-644389	#25857465

B. "Includes" statements

1. Ohio official reports (Cincinnati, Ohio : Advance sheets)	sn82-5967	#8610029
2. Bio-base	87-643356	#5214949
3. Japan artistique	83-646228	#9987785
4. The Musical mercury	sc83-7078	#9119421
5. Bulletin of the International Social Security Association	56-15865	#1771735
6. Labor relations reference manual	39-10217	#1755409

7.	The Source book of American state legislation	82-642083	#6181988
8.	Euskal urtekari estatistikoa	84-640037	#10260281
9.	California. Dept. of Water Resources. Transactions under the Davis-Grunsky Act	sc84-7050	#1552399
10.	InfoTrac	92-644672	#22288636
11.	Electronic clipper	96-647358	#34187454
12.	International directory of wildland fire (Diskette)	sn96-47055	#34998257
13.	Data report of oceanographic observations	sn96-47069	#35106961
14.	Refworld (CD-ROM)	sn96-47049	#34926272
15.	Morbidity and mortality weekly report (Online)	sn96-47012	#34197054
16.	Compact disc Code of Federal Regulations. E, H & S updated as of . . .	95-645829	#33097541
17.	All of MacTech magazine, CD-ROM	sn94-20494	#30889715
18.	Earth surface processes and landforms	81-643477	#6160332
19.	World*data	sn95-43275	#32035140
20.	Synthesis	76-16575	#1430237

C. Proceedings information

1.	Current trends in life sciences	sf83-2017	#7087481
2.	Advances in biomaterials	sf83-2004	#6832932
3.	Advances in myocardiology	80-643989	#6353133
4.	Washington State Entomological Society. Proceedings of the Washington State Entomological Society	82-646578	#1663476
5.	Advances in data base theory	sn82-20071	#7399682
6.	Developments in food carbohydrate	83-640905	#4532240
7.	Conference on Application of X-ray Analysis. Advances in x-ray analysis	82-642132	#1461274
8.	Fracture mechanics of ceramics Analysis. Advances in x-ray analysis	83-641076	#4298543
9.	Clinical science. Supplement	sn80-2765	#6297497
10.	Australian mining and petroleum law journal	82-643157	#7065636
11.	Publications of the Texas Folk-lore Society	16-6413	#1767350
12.	American journal of physiology	a43-3158	#1480180

D. General coverage information

1.	Labor market information for affirmative action programs (Virginia Employment Commission. Manpower Research Division). Supplement	83-640504	#7066166

2. Serie encuestas. Opinión empresarial del sector industrial — 82-645023 — #8712564
3. Curriculum development library. Cumulative index — sn83-10187 — #6677031
4. Ingreso y producto, Puerto Rico — 77-640669 — #3278795
5. Costs of producing livestock in the United States — 82-642804 — #8363496
6. Iowa. Dept. of Transportation. Planning and research program — 82-646782 — #7438797
7. National Research Council (U.S.). Issues and studies — 82-647078 — #8605610
8. Magill's cinema annual — 83-644357 — #9315435
9. South Pacific bibliography — 84-641270 — #9921005
10. Art book review — 83-643065 — #8758334
11. Shichōson ni okeru chiiki seisaku no dōkō no gaiyō — 83-642823 — #9439803
12. Oregon. Dept. of Education. Career and Vocational Education Section. Planning for vocational education in Oregon — 82-642268 — #8957504
13. Indice de ciências socials — 85-640238 — #5973286
14. Guide to U.S. government maps. Geologic and hydrologic maps — 85-650190 — #4660069
15. Trademarkscan. U.S., state — #34629672

E. General translation notes

1. Khimiiâ i tekhnologiiâ vody — 83-644945 — #8558750
2. Soviet sports review — 82-647330 — #5214378
3. Chinese sociology and anthropology — 77-4280 — #1548629
4. Chinese physics — 81-643627 — #7052624
5. Mapping sciences and remote sensing — 85-641130 — #11120779
6. Bibliography of modern Hebrew literature in translation — 81-644248 — #6038553

NOTES ABOUT TITLES

A. Source of the title

1. The Arachnet electronic journal on virtual culture — 95-647863 — #27763895
2. Wisconsin. Emergency Number Systems Board. Annual report on the operations of the 911 Emergency Numbers Systems Board in Wisconsin — 82-644709 — #8673093
3. Entertainment law journal (Entertainment Law Journal Association) — sc82-6830 — #8141124

4. Katei zasshi	83-645830	#9921382
5. Court opinions reference disc	sn96-4298	#35163305
6. Open letter	cn76-300161	#2096108
7. Data report of oceanographic observations	sn96-47069	#35106961
8. J.UCS		#35834978
9. Music theory online	sn92-6794	#27188803

B. Title proper information

1. Analysis geoeconomico		#9348577
2. Compensation (Washington, D.C. : 1982)	82-645698	#8370349
3. Faglige bidrag	75-644078	#4354330
4. Getting results for the hands-on manager. C	sn96-30169	#35655887
5. Honpō keizai tōkei	28-30743	#2239062
6. Bulletin (Holmes Safety Association)	82-643960	#5140851
7. Oral History Association. Membership directory	sc80-1274	#5266585
8. A Journal of female liberation	sc80-826	#1754586
9. Chilton's I & C S	83-646306	#9673774
10. International directory of wildland fire (Diskette)	sn96-47055	#34998257
11. TESS	sn96-47043	#34742135
12. Current facts	sn96-47022	#25597220

C. Miscellaneous title information

1. Försäkringstidningen (Stockholm, Sweden)	61-45524	#9462767
2. National woodlands	sf93-94709	#7085730
3. Case and comment	sn82-7976	#8789037
4. Öl und Kohle	sn83-5728	#9659417
5. Fortschritte auf dem Gebiete der Röntgenstrahlen und der Nuklearmedizin. Ergänzungsband	sf84-1046	#1644093
6. Education policy analysis archives	sn93-7169	#27483741
7. Studies in formative spirituality	84-641552	#5156328

D. Language of title/parallel title information

1. Lingvaj problemoj kaj lingvo-planado	sn80-8496	#3805689
2. Education. Whites	82-643935	#8560925
3. Community health in SA	sc84-1095	#10106139
4. Belgium. Parlement. Parlementaire documentatie	83-640944	#9189536
5. Education. Whites	82-643935	#8560925

6.	Études de statistique agricole		#2927584
7.	Groundwater series (Pretoria)	sf83-9020	#2361386
8.	Regionalstatistik årbog	86-644844	#8291363
9.	Annales entomologici fennici		#6134600
10.	South African Library Association Jaarverslag	sc82-2493	#8801326
11.	Filatelist	82-646932	#9014917
12.	Technical report (Skipjack Survey and Assessment Programme)	sn83-10411	#8541060
13.	Ingreso y producto, Puerto Rico	77-640669	#3278795
14.	Nepāla (Kathmandu, Nepal)	82-647210	#9059433
15.	Bibliografía ecuatoriana	77-649113	#4432658
16.	Electric power in Canada	73-645063	#1787807
17.	International medieval bibliography (CD-ROM)	sn96-47046	#34847071

E. Names of titles within a serial (not issued separately)

1.	Baldwin's Ohio tax service	83-640560	#6480527
2.	Dr. A. Petermann's Mitteilungen aus Justus Perthes' geographischer Anstalt	sf83-6896	#5860725
3.	Health, United States	76-641496	#3151554
4.	Coin & medal news	83-641852	#8302946
5.	The Nautical almanac for the year	sc79-2685	#1286390
6.	Serials in the British Library (Annual)	sn84-10171	#8264921
7.	Garden supply retailer	82-645629	#5303894
8.	Academy of Accounting Historians. Membership roster		#6865903
9.	The Arachnet electronic journal on virtual culture	95-647863	#27763895

F. Varying forms of title

1.	United States. Office of Management and Budget. Budget of the United States government	70-611049	#932137
2.	Rede Ferroviária Federal (Brazil) Relatório anual	83-641830	#5141169
3.	Oil & petrochemical pollution	84-642414	#9250569
4.	The South Central bulletin	83-642124	#2740893
5.	Current trends in life sciences	sf83-2017	#7087481
6.	Ethnic racial brotherhood	80-641850	#6525120
7.	Bibliografía ecuatoriana	77-649113	#4432658
8.	Golden Gate University. School of Law. Golden Gate University law review	sn82-7120	#9034010
9.	Knitting times	74-645022	#1794210

10.	Zambia. Central Statistical Office. National accounts . . . and input-output table	82-640310	#5753666
11.	Haiku Bungakkan kiyo	83-641935	#9310213
12.	State government research checklist	sn79-4788	#4736514

G. Alternate issues

1.	Abstracts of Bulgarian scientific literature. Geosciences	81-641638	#6799592
2.	ASHRAE handbook		#8009578
3.	Early child development and care: ECDC	82-640509	#1772625
4.	Modern brewery age	sn81-5449	#6392377

IMPRINT VARIATION INFORMATION

1.	Camera lucida	83-646300	#6430212
2.	Letras femeninas	81-642380	#3816008
3.	Advances in cladistics	83-646412	#9820449
4.	Boston Society of Landscape Architects. Annual report	sc82-4345	#8412345
5.	Beiträge zur Volkskunde der Ungardeutschen	sc83-8037	#9104157
6.	Alcheringa (New York, N.Y.)	72-626511	#1780749
7.	Decorative art and modern interiors	sc83-3099	#1781874
8.	Congress on Research in Dance. CORD newsletter	sc82-2282	#8530503
9.	Federal communications law journal		#35003921

ISSUING INFORMATION

A. Physical description

1.	Biblioinformación cafetera	sn82-22195	#4738783
2.	Peasant studies newsletter	sn83-10622	#1963832
3.	Encyclopédie permanente, Japan	82-640488	#6344244
4.	National sales tax rate directory	82-646612	#8342190
5.	America buys: Updating service	sn82-22060	#7570064
6.	Employee benefits cases	81-642948	#7033880
7.	Oregon Land Use Board of Appeals decisions	80-70149	#7064196
8.	Collected original resources in education		#3250843
9.	Flue	sc82-4472	#8150495
10.	Bibliographic guide to law	79-642569	#2282334
11.	Library of Congress. Subject headings in microform	79-641066	#3454199
12.	Whisper	sn95-7498	#33118850

B. Updates and revisions

1.	Maps on file	sn81-791	#7240499
2.	Pay scales in the California state civil service	46-27570	#8880233
3.	Uniform crime reports for the United States	30-27005	#2165904
4.	A Bibliography of ab initio molecular wave functions. Supplement for . . .	82-646873	#8301811
5.	Eurostatistik	80-648763	#5144628
6.	Automotive literature index	82-643376	#7289023
7.	Labor-management relations in the public service	81-645131	#5191433
8.	A List of references: maize virus and mycoplasma diseases	sc85-8271	#7541620
9.	Bureau of National Affairs (Washington, D.C.). Environmental reporter. Federal laws		#3373471

C. Miscellaneous issuing information

1.	Mukashi	83-646483	#10028803
2.	Indiana Stream Pollution Control Board. State of Indiana water pollution control program plan	83-645852	#6934812
3.	Electronic publishing abstracts	84-642000	#9960391
4.	Annual survey of family law	83-641536	#7702984
5.	The Annual of the British School at Athens	19-19615	#1537363
6.	American Helicopter Society. Annual forum proceedings	sn82-21296	#7315648
7.	Direction of trade statistics	81-649851	#7154584
8.	Building services & environmental engineer	sn82-22261	#5249236
9.	Godishnik na Visshiâ institut po arkhitektura i stroitelstvo, Sofiâ	82-647154	#8162066
10.	Disabled USA	77-643096	#3322866
11.	NOAA technical report NMFS SSRF	83-644784	#1522427
12.	Transportation safety information report	81-641374	#5166195
13.	Bulletin (California. Dept. of Water Resources)	sf96-10000	#1213170
14.	Getting results for the hands-on manager. C	sn96-30169	#35655887

MISCELLANEOUS GENERAL NOTES

1.	Abbay	80-646507	#6825901
2.	Frauenberuf (Weimar, Germany)	sf94-92064	#7338884

3.	Journal of studies on alcohol	sc83-7250	#5916226
4.	Annales de physique	49-52171	#1481283
5.	Cuadernos panamericanos de información geográfica	sn83-10763	#8247530
6.	Suid-Afrika se kommersiële houtbronne	82-646953	#7603824
7.	Current developments in copyright law	82-642095	#4279222
8.	Science, technology, and American diplomacy (Washington, D.C. : 1980)	81-640299	#6742417
9.	Le Guide arabe pour le commerce, l'industrie & les professions libérales dans les pays arabes	53-32838	#3819945
10.	Handbook for employees transferring to Spain	sn83-10354	#7261042
11.	Farmer cooperatives	76-646745	#2200788
12	Annual bulletin of housing and building statistics for Europe	60-2123	#1261977
13.	Demographic yearbook	50-641	#1168223
14.	Current industrial reports	82-645446	#2547072
15.	Journal of geophysical research	83-641459	#3918314
16.	Hoy (Santiago, Chile : 1977)	78-646252	#4181058
17.	Complete desk reference of veterinary pharmaceuticals & biologicals (Media, Pa.)	sn82-20903	#5933707
18.	National Academy of Sciences (U.S.). Proceedings of the National Academy of Sciences of the United States of America	16-10069	#1607201
19.	California yearbook (California Almanac Company)	82-645580	#4758346
20.	Progress in the prevention and control of air pollution in . . .	82-646574	#2902992

DESCRIPTION BASED ON NOTES

1.	Leading U.S. corporations	sn81-6206	#6352772
2.	Asia-Pacific exchange journal	sn94-3726	#30698706
3.	Armadillo culture		#31491416
4.	APSRS	sn95-20078	#32315307
5.	Cambridge structural database system	sn96-47038	#34331851
6.	Journal of molecular biology (Online)	sn96-47032	#34479722
7.	SAE J-finder	sn96-47044	#34764038
8.	Current facts	sn96-47022	#25597220
9.	Applied physics letters online	sn96-4285	#34787267

EDITORS

1.	Encyclopedia of associations	76-46129	#1223579
2.	Meanderings	sn96-44079	#31692720

3. RIF/T   #30697128
4. British union-catalogue of periodicals   66-1557   #2049137

504 BIBLIOGRAPHY, ETC. NOTE

1. Publications of the Texas Folk-lore   16-6413   #1767350
   Society
2. Annales historiques de la Révolution   34-18456   #1481323
   française

506 RESTRICTIONS ON ACCESS NOTE

1. Journal of molecular biology (Online)   sn96-47032   #34479722
2. International mathematics research   sn96-38116   #34987691
   notices (Online)

508 CREATION/PRODUCTION CREDITS NOTE

Examples taken from *CONSER Editing Guide*, 1994 ed.

510 CITATION/REFERENCES NOTE

1. The Community services catalyst   92-662137   #3334057
2. Educom review   92-650221   #19588058
3. IEEE transactions on education   64-974   #1752549

511 PARTICIPANT OR PERFORMER NOTE

Examples taken from *CONSER Editing Guide*, 1994 ed.

513 TYPE OF REPORT AND PERIOD COVERED NOTE

Examples taken from *CONSER Editing Guide*, 1994 ed.

515 NUMBERING PECULIARITIES NOTE

REPORT YEAR COVERAGE

1. Botswana. Ministry of Finance and   82-642148   #8401470
   Development Planning. National
   development plan

2.	Current industrial reports. MQ-C1, Survey of plant capacity	81-649750	#3811904
3.	Gumma Kenritsu Rekishi Hakubutsukan. Gumma Kenritsu Rekishi Hakubutsukan nempō	82-643434	#8482883
4.	Istituto universitario navale (Naples, Italy). Annuario	82-640015	#7602647
5.	A Financial analysis of the for-hire tank truck industry for the year . . .	sc83-1049	#3808610
6.	U.S.-Japan Cooperative Cancer Research Program. Progress report	83-640506	#4750211
7.	Société anonyme Cockerill-Ougrée. Report and accounts presented at the general meeting of shareholders	sc83-4030	#9032637
8.	Illinois. Office of the State Treasurer. Treasurer's semi-annual report	83-640271	#9135474
9.	Citrus fruits by states . . .	82-642464	#8320201
10.	National Foundation for Infantile Paralysis. Annual report	sf82-8043	#1605984
11.	Equalized assessed valuations and tax rates	sn83-10251	#8163438
12.	Monthly Florida motor gasoline consumption	84-640160	#10344654
13.	Statistics (New Mexico. Dept. of Finance and Administration. Office of Education)	79-643332	#5121099
14.	Report of funds granted to Delaware during fiscal year . . . by State agency and by Federal program (OMB number)	82-646944	#9021855
15.	Ireland. National Board for Science and Technology. Annual report for the year ended 31 Dec. . . .	82-644179	#8602620
16.	Montréal (Québec). Annual report	82-644940	#6679961
17.	Maryland. Criminal Justice Information Advisory Board. Annual report to the Governor and the General Assembly	82-646410	#8925147
18.	Connecticut. Office of Policy & Management. Statewide facility and capital plan	81-646396	#7636440
19.	United States. Environmental Data Service. International decade of ocean exploration	78-644884	#2679186
20.	InfoTrac	92-644672	#22288636
21.	Magazine index plus	sn94-15265	#31619759
22.	NewsBank reference service plus	sn94-26017	#29557368
23.	The AGRICOLA database	sn95-43802	#22296080

DOUBLE NUMBERING

1.	Videha	73-904759	#8014499
2.	Domestic engineering and the journal of mechanical contracting	sf84-1000	#1781876
3.	Mexico. President. State of the nation report to the Mexican Congress	83-645133	#8267448
4.	L'Information grammaticale	sc82-4499	#8919780
5.	Arkansas. State Board for Vocational Education. Arkansas annual plan for vocational education, PL94-482	83-640850	#5516335
7.	East and west (Rome, Italy)	56-33103	#1567218
8.	Analele Universității București. Acta logica	sc83-3075	#3507383
9.	The Bellingham review	82-644979	#3689085
10.	Il Nuovo cimento della Società italiana di fisica. D, Condensed matter, atomic, molecular and chemical physics, biophysics	sc82-3630	#8724239
11.	Alabama medicaid	82-646241	#9035826
12.	Acta oecologica. Oecologia plantarum	81-645733	#6257682
13.	Classical antiquity	83-640320	#7870789
14.	Isotope geoscience	85-645271	#9428986
15.	American Council on Education studies. Series VI, Student personnel work	39-15476	#3511884
16.	Journal of the Chemical Society. Faraday transactions I	sn79-4663	#1034405
17.	American Philosophical Society. Proceedings of the American Philosophical Society	sn78-683	#9292549
18.	UFSI reports	84-648940	#7939882
19.	United States. National Commission for Employment Policy. Annual report to the President and the Congress of the National Commission for Employment Policy	80-648291	#6564180
20.	Allergy supplementum	sc83-2189	#9232400
21.	The New York Jewish week	83-642782	#9144716
22.	al-Wa'y al-Islāmī	ne68-4659	#2178455
23.	Cambridge structural database system	sn96-47038	#34331851
24.	Scholar (New York, N.Y.)	sn92-3649	#25061433

COMBINED ISSUES OR VOLUMES

1.	Current industrial reports. M25E, Mattresses, foundations and sleep furniture	sc93-20587	#3081040

2.	Papers of the New World Archaeological Foundation	60-41468	#1142787
3.	Art and poetry today	78-914394	#5817473
4.	Acta mathematica Academiae Scientiarum Hungaricae	54-20368	#1460914
5.	European file	84-651518	#5211930
6.	Community mental health review	79-643403	#2381437
7.	Artpark	82-642102	#3819051
8.	The Florida genealogist	82-646389	#3957742
9.	Afro American journal of philosophy	84-644990	#10149260
10.	Indiana University. The President's report	52-62053	#8717702
11.	Chemical dependencies	81-640950	#7111945
12.	Svobodnoe slovo (Mount Vernon, N.Y.)	82-644421	#8412883
13.	Ethnic racial brotherhood	80-641850	#6525120

NUMBERING INCONSISTENCIES OR IRREGULARITIES

A. Numbering lacking

1.	Hans David Billman family bulletin	83-642404	#9372683
2.	Bulletin du Centre d'études et de recherche scientifiques	62-58596	#9347914
3.	Desertification control	82-643809	#8543455
4.	The Numbers news	sc82-4133	#7757812
5.	73 (Brooklyn, N.Y.)	63-28249	#1774754
6.	Japanese religions	83-645874	#6548536
7.	Geosur	82-643195	#8427052
8.	Market Technicians Association journal	82-645234	#8744678
9.	Flue	sc82-4472	#8150495
10.	Leading U.S. corporations	sn81-6206	#6352772
11.	Bibliografía latinoamericana. 1, Trabajos publicados por latino americanos en revistas extranjeras	84-640870	#10353036
12.	Bulletin (British Guiana. Geological Survey)	sf82-8049	#1287373
13.	Beiträge zur Gerontologie und Altenarbeit	sf85-4045	#9870807
14.	Early modern Europe today	sn83-10761	#8774049
15.	Materialy po geneticheskoĭ eksperimental'noĭ mineralogy	66-49173	#2617230
16.	Evaluation	73-640899	#1784879
17.	Itinerario	sn83-10746	#5624669
18.	New road . . .	a43-3687	#2409801
19.	The Virginia economic review	84-642766	#1550102

B. Numbering dropped
   1. Design engineering (London, England)   82-640070   #6237037
   2. U.S.-Japan Cooperative Cancer   83-640506   #4750211
      Research Program. Progress report
   3. Journal of economic studies (Glasgow,   82-645768   #1001112
      Scotland)
   4. Communist (Chicago, Ill.)   81-649127   #4675593
   5. Disabled USA   77-643096   #3322866
   6. Skyscraper management   ca33-801   #1765613
   7. Eurostat-CD   sn95-43273   #32211051
   8. Aperture (San Francisco, Calif.)   58-30845   #1481673

C. Numbering added
   1. Monthly Detroit   83-640481   #3524336
   2. EDIS   79-640361   #4359560
   3. The Pierre-Fort Pierre Genealogical   83-642845   #9445548
      Society
   4. Research proceedings (University   82-913340   #3863839
      of Delhi. Dept. of Anthropology)
   5. International railway journal and rapid   81-641150   #6070542
      transit review
   6. Metropolitan Life Insurance Company.   31-30794   #1757228
      Statistical bulletin

D. Numbering errors
   1. Transactions of the Indiana State   sc82-1366   #7065529
      Medical Society
   2. Critical mass energy journal   sn81-4626   #7136089
   3. Le Praticien. Supplément au no . . .   sc82-4474   #8852991
   4. Garden supply retailer   82-645629   #5303894
   5. Family therapy   73-640444   #1731055
   6. Modern brewery age   sn81-5449   #6392377
   7. The Field artilleryman   83-642607   #9399559
   8. Illinois. Dept. of Mines and Minerals.   sc80-1080   #2371496
      Coal report of Illinois
   9. N.A.R.D. journal   12-25705   #1695474
   10. The Progressive   33-15217   #1762985
   11. The Candle of Phi Upsilon Omicron   #5130878
   12. Ebony   52-42074   #1567306
   13. Education directory. Colleges &   83-645625   #2575450
      universities
   14. Analele Universiţăţii Bucureşti. Seria   66-47376   #8909820
      acta logica
   15. Abrasive Engineering Society (U.S.).   82-645670   #6296946
      Conference/Exhibition. Proceedings

16.	The Ampleforth review	sc82-4469	#5539960
17.	National Association of Retail Druggists (U.S.). N.A.R.D. newsletter	78-645112	#4102933
18.	Employment hours and earnings, Virginia	82-645932	#7766075
19.	Municipal review & AMA news	82-647392	#7386722
20.	Urban planning reports	sc82-1368	#6829048
21.	The NAHB news	83-641518	#7912857
22.	Wen i (Hong Kong)	82-647228	#7839743
23.	Journal of the Inter-American Foundation	82-646994	#4862949
24.	Indiana. Laws of the State of Indiana, passed at the . . . session of the General Assembly	07-31549	#8733001

E. Numbering shared with other titles

1.	Brief		#1537076
2.	Domestic cars mechanical parts/labor estimating guide	81-643746	#7434866
3.	Transactions of the Society of Petroleum Engineers of the American Institute of Mining, Metallurgical, and Petroleum Engineers, Inc.	85-647411	#2461356
4.	Ferroelectrics. Letters section	87-655586	#8209340
5.	American studies international	76-649667	#2077111
6.	Acta pathological et microbiological Scandinavica. Supplement	sc83-3060	#7339040
7.	Mutation research. Mutation research letters	sn81-3918	#7356055
8.	DLA bulletin (Electronic version)	sn94-3597	#29905912

F. Numbering that does not begin with vol. 1

1.	Québec (Province). Régie du logement. Décisions de la Régie du logement	84-641958	#10521046
2.	Urban outlook	sc82-1294	#8445335
3.	Ukrainian mathematical journal	sf78-501	#1496592
4.	Today's education. Mathematics/science edition	81-643036	#6840763
5.	Le Praticien. Supplément au no . . .	sc82-4474	#8852991
6.	Adansonia	sf82-4090	#1461074
7.	Journal of experimental psychology. Human learning and memory	76-643081	#1172614
8.	International yearbook of education	49-48323	#1753766
9.	Journal de physique. Lettres	sn81-4452	#1318711
10.	Deutsche optische Wochenschrift und Central-Zeitung für Optik und Mechanik (Docentra)	sf83-1012	#8828735

11.	Bollettino dens Unione matematica Italiana. C, Analisi funzionale e applicazioni	sn83-10601	#7880785
12.	American archives of rehabilitation therapy	sn80-1695	#1479313
13.	Boletin de Instituto Español de Oceanografía (1977)	82-645020	#8714537
14.	Colección estudios CIEPLAN	82-646207	#6175141

G. Inconsistencies in chronological designations

1.	Branka	82-646905	#9013181
2.	Common stock indexes	sc82-4481	#8417735
3.	The Arup journal	sc83-7004	#8838510
4.	Art west	83-643043	#4543340
5.	Douglas County Illinois Genealogical Society	83-647615	#10176466
6.	Estatística básica de arrecadação	83-642491	#6765943
7.	The Field artilleryman	83-642607	#9399559
8.	American Association of Exporters and Importers. Membership directory	sn84-10436	#8329516
9.	Les Annales de la recherche urbaine	91-650750	#5856529
10.	Directory of employee organizations in New York State	76-620003	#5093230
11.	Bridge (Belgrade, Serbia)	66-9922	#2652059
12.	The Register of the American Saddlebred Horse Association (incorporated)	82-647022	#8264831

H. Miscellaneous numbering inconsistencies or irregularities

1.	The JAG journal	52-66952	#1449089
2.	Design book review	83-646132	#9361004
3.	Calendar (California Debt Advisory Commission)	sc84-8099	#10068625
4.	Boletim mensal (Banco de Fomento Nacional)	82-647030	#9033750
5.	Soviet Union	51-36672	#1642588
6.	Soviet soil science	61-675	#1587583
7.	Commission of the European Communities. Directorate-General for Agriculture. Newsletter on the common agricultural policy		#5794632
8.	Directory information service	77-641771	#3208182
9.	The Economic bulletin of Ghana	67-122046	#8186026
10.	Publications of the American Statistical Association		#1680935

11. Jen min wen hsüeh	83-648239	#1605226
12. New guard bulletin	83-645987	#4811308
13. Sverkhtverdye materialy	84-642684	#9820773
14. A Rand note	sn83-10953	#5183244
15. Journal of geophysical research. Space physics	83-641459	#3918314
16. Official airline guide (North American ed.)	sc83-9407	#1077891
17. Book review digest	06-24490	#6038062
18. Modern brewery age	sn81-5449	#6392377
19. Classical rag (Silver Spring, Md.)	83-640269	#9135086
20. Joint Computer Conference. Proceedings of the . . . Joint Computer Conference	55-44701	#4683874
21. Ancestors west	82-645233	#8744728
22. Current facts	sn96-47022	#25597220
23. InterJournal	sn95-4550	#31989568

ISSUING PECULIARITIES

A. General issuing peculiarities

1. Comparative studies	82-643523	#7869905
2. Keynote (New York, N.Y. : 1883)	sc83-7085	#2448119
3. Bulletin (California. Dept. of Water Resources)	sf96-10000	#1213170
4. Pubblicazioni dell'Osservatorio "G. Horn d'Arturo"	sc82-3652	#8905607
5. Montana. Legislature. Senate and House journals of the . . . Legislature of the State of Montana commencing in special session . . . and ending . . .	82-645227	#8744637
6. ICP software directory (1981)	82-647332	#8074041
7. Bulletin signalétique. 225, Tectonique, géophysique interne	83-641972	#8327316
8. The Eastern economist (New Delhi, India : 1943)	49-20208	#1567281
9. Occupational health & safety (Waco, Tex.)	82-641424	#2214952
10. United States. Bureau of Radiological Health. Office of the Associate Director for Administration. Technical Information Staff. Bureau of Radiological Health publications index	79-642649	#4430580
11. Academy of Accounting Historians. Working paper series		#4874242
12. Ch'ōngsaekchi	83-641378	#9228280

13.	Annex 21	sn82-22044	#8568502
14.	Newsletter (Scientists' Center for Animal Welfare (Washington, D.C.))	sc83-8343	#9384415
15.	Meridians 12-23	82-641387	#7906012
16.	Advances in psychology (Amsterdam, Netherlands)	sf83-1005	#5253350
17.	Arnoldia, Zimbabwe Rhodesia	85-642372	#8223338
18.	Industrial Relations Research Association. Membership directory of the Industrial Relations Research Association	sn82-20931	#5812981
19.	Summary of legislative action on the budget bill	84-644172	#8732677
20.	Progress toward regulatory reform	sc83-1312	#9086578
21.	Annales d'immunologie	sn80-13574	#1643402
22.	Analytical letters	sn80-45	#1481079
23.	Management science	sf84-19092	#4827722
24.	The Biochemical journal	26-11128	#1532962
25.	Washington University (Saint Louis, Mo.). Washington University studies	18-8774	#1644739
26.	USSR report. Life sciences. Effect of nonionizing electromagnetic radiation (Public ed.)	sc83-3009	#8525784
27.	Progress in planning	83-640193	#1049759
28.	Bibliographic index of health education periodicals	82-646381	#7754004
29.	Magazine index plus	sn94-15265	#31619759
30.	Development (Cambridge, England : Online)	sn96-4702	#34506804
31.	Chicago journal of theoretical computer science	sn93-4456	#29297160
32.	NewsBank reference service plus	sn94-26017	#29557368

B. Number of issues per volume, etc.

1.	Biochemistry international	81-649182	#6748187
2.	Chemical geology	77-3539	#1553973
3.	Monographs on music, dance, and theatre in Asia	83-640375	#9150653
4.	Environmental pollution. Series A, Ecological and biological	81-643637	#6067650
5.	Urban affairs papers	83-644053	#6460674
6.	Social security bulletin (Washington, D.C. : 1938). Annual statistical supplement	sc77-385	#1939422

7.	Current industrial reports. M25E, Mattresses, foundations and sleep furniture	81-649769	#3081040
8.	Tōyō Bunko (Japan). Tōyō Bunko nenpō	sc82-3673	#8921273
9.	Career education quarterly	81-641275	#4571463

C. Issued in named parts, sections, etc.

1.	California state rail plan	sc82-6153	#8922519
2.	Global banking directory	82-646200	#8913588
3.	American history	82-643952	#8231094
4.	Local area personal income	80-641946	#3622072
5.	National accounts (Organisation for Economic Co-operation and Development. Dept. of Economics and Statistics)	sc84-8563	#9420508
6.	The . . . Study of media and markets	sc82-7498	#7233459
7.	Directory of Soviet officials	84-640183	#2197616
8.	United States. United States code annotated	95-660894	#33039263

D. Issued in unnamed parts, sections, etc.

1.	Associations' publications in print	81-17005	#8008221
2.	Ethnic information sources of the United States	84-640146	#9536958
3.	Online database search services directory	84-642259	#10062770
4.	Directory of American scholars	57-9125	#1246775
5.	Industriens struktur og aktiviteter	83-645632	#7058185
6.	GeoSciTech citation index	83-642674	#8297273
7.	Annual communications law institute	82-641723	#8166137
8.	American Institute of Architects AIA journal	46-21775	#4368512
9.	Geological Society of America bulletin	87-644643	#1570691
10.	Allgemeine deutsche Bibliothek	07-23735	#1479144
11.	Arctic Institute of North America. Library. Catalogue. Supplement	75-646581	#4265207
12.	Avery Library. Catalog of the Avery Memorial Architectural Library of Columbia University. 2d ed., enlarged. Supplement	75-649442	#2244927
13.	North central North Dakota genealogical record	83-640311	#8147331
14.	Hoppea	83-640249	#9129932

15.	Bell & Howell Co. Indexing Center. Bell & Howell's newspaper index to the Washington post	80-640592	#5972290
16.	Situación de la oferta de vivienda en España en . . .	82-641815	#8275919
17.	American Institute for Decision Sciences. Meeting. Proceedings	82-646173	#1667466
18.	al-Arshīf al-suhufī	82-645613	#8815992
19.	Register for earned income taxes	82-647165	#9055107
20.	Catalogue des thèses et écrits académiques	83-642231	#6445170
21.	ASTM standards source	96-647355	#34187408
22.	Moody's international annual reports	sn96-380139	#34948695
23.	SAE J-finder	sn96-47044	#34764038
24.	Pressdok	sn91-28014	#23132733
25.	SciDex cumulative index	92-645935	#26829789

E. Multiple or revised editions

1.	The Poetical register, and repository of fugitive poetry for . . .	12-22988	#2266289
2.	Basic (Pell) grant validation handbook	81-642713	#7616530
3.	Chronicle vocational school manual	82-643014	#7320922
4.	Colorado air quality data report	82-646887	#8877767
5.	United States. Dept. of Energy. Congressional budget request	80-643192	#4837750
6.	Directory of Soviet officials	84-640183	#2197616
7.	Imported collision estimating guide	81-642225	#7546402

F. Cumulations

1.	Advance annotation service to the Code of Virginia	sc83-9199	#7921297
2.	Federal immigration law reporter	sn89-5800	#9293065
3.	Food bibliography	83-644044	#6688720
4.	Catalogue of British official publications not published by HMSO	84-647868	#7678038
5.	The Forum index	83-648059	#9674340
6.	Cartel (Austin, Tex.)	84-642461	#2256041
7.	The Foundation Center source book profiles	77-79015	#3718433
8.	Text-Index	sc83-5028	#7789814
9.	Artikelbasen	sn96-32079	#33670510
10.	NewsBank reference service plus	sn94-26017	#29557368
11.	Science citation index	92-644531	#20113418

PRELIMINARY ISSUES

1.	Contemporary orthopaedics	sc83-1114	#5057206
2.	South (London, England)	84-645374	#7309028
3.	EC trade with the ACP states and the south Mediterranean states	82-647311	#5968193
4.	Garden design	82-647188	#8610163
5.	Newsletter on education and training programmes for specialized information personnel	sn82-20047	#5533585
6.	Computer business news	sc83-8104	#4181247
7.	Automation news (New York, N.Y.)	sc83-8566	#9114303
8.	Quality progress	sc83-8122	#6569242
9.	Assessors journal	70-3958	#1514495
10.	Doctoral dissertations in history	77-640363	#2429011
11.	Art digest/South newsletter	sn82-20227	#3855229
12.	America, history and life	64-25630	#1479243
13.	Weeds world	sn95-15551	#33893098

SUSPENSION OF PUBLICATION

1.	The Dance journal	82-643577	#4877180
2.	Maritime	73-11160	#1756696
3.	Trade union information	57-24345	#6201585
4.	Writings on American history	04-8590	#1770230
5.	Maryland free press (Hagerstown, Md.)	sn84-26707	#10663331

ITEMS NOT PUBLISHED

1.	EAR	sc82-3313	#6887600
2.	Evaluation and change	sc82-8179	#6504146
3.	AV guide	sc83-1140	#3867076
4.	FAO commodity review and outlook	a63-278	#2720294
5.	Annales de géographie	sn79-9782	#3341949
6.	Cleveland Electrical/Electronics Conference and Exposition. CECON . . . record	84-643223	#5098134
7.	Conference on Application of X-ray Analysis. Advances in x-ray analysis	82-642132	#1461274
8.	Association of Collegiate Schools of Architecture. Proceedings of the ACSA annual meeting	80-643592	#5384757
9.	Accademia nazionale dei Lincei. Annuario della Accademia nazionale dei Lincei	52-28690	#6340475
10.	Journal of American insurance	sf89-91048	#5692000
11.	Beadle's popular library		#8357938

| 12. | Bulletin signalétique. 354, Maladies de l'appareil digestif, chirurgie abdominale | 73-642399 | #1071291 |

516 TYPE OF COMPUTER FILE OR DATA NOTE

1.	Computer-mediated communication magazine	sn94-2066	#30373620
2.	Library of Congress. Cataloging Directorate. LC cataloging newsline	95-660725	#27076319
3.	Apicultural information and issues (Online)	95-647858	#32207891
4.	EDsearch	96-660502	#32804455
5.	Artikelbasen	sn96-32079	#33670510
6.	Hua-hsia wen chai	sn95-42471	#33397925
7.	Nezavisimaiâ gazeta (Moscow, Russia : Online)	sn96-47017	#34294234
8.	Electronic clipper	96-647358	#34187454
9.	TESL-EJ	95-649669	#28945546
10.	United States. Navy. Navy news service	95-649666	#31042981
11.	Stata	sn96-47867	#35648344

520 SUMMARY, ETC. NOTE

1.	Academe this week	sn95-33852	#32808359
2.	Architectural publications index on disc	sn96-23120	#33072688
3.	Artikelbasen	sn96-32079	#33670510
4.	Bean bag	sn95-15560	#31494031
5.	Technical note (Forest Engineering Research Institute of Canada)	cn80-39014	#3418077
6.	Moody's international annual reports	sn96-380139	#34948695
7.	The Wall Street journal ondisc	sn92-22996	#25809149
8.	Intellectual property (San Francisco, Calif.)	sn95-29372	#33939562
9.	Directory of European lawyers (Floppy disk)	95-652208	#33312117
10.	Web journal of current legal issues		#34986084
11.	Char-koosta news (CD-ROM)		#32884188
12.	LymeNet newsletter		#34781292
13.	Pressdok	95-645763	#29233645
14.	USGS peak values. United States	sn92-19480	#26391828
15.	USAPAT	96-660804	#31190600
16.	NBC News transcripts ondisc	95-655237	#32485197

521 TARGET AUDIENCE NOTE

Examples taken from *CONSER Editing Guide*, 1994 ed.

522 GEOGRAPHIC COVERAGE NOTE

Examples taken from *CONSER Editing Guide*, 1994 ed.

525 SUPPLEMENT NOTE

UNNAMED SUPPLEMENTS

1. Zoologische Jahrbücher. Abteilung für Systematik, Ökologie und Geographie der Tiere — 82-645525 — #1770666
2. Hudson communiqué — sc83-2320 — #8448188
3. The Proletarian line — 79-915582 — #8655665
4. Neurobehavioral toxicology and teratology — 81-642303 — #7088111
5. Bio-bibliografía boliviana — 79-648775 — #3020266
6. The Arup journal — sc83-7004 — #8838510
7. GeoJournal — 78-642013 — #3693750
8. Chandigarh (India : Union Ter.) Chandigarh Administration gazette — 78-645952 — #8363808
9. World aviation directory — 40-11496 — #2413063
10. Czechoslovakia. Ministerstvo zdravotnictví. Věstník Ministerstva zdravotnictví — 67-59180 — #5080127
11. New Zealand Dairy Board. Annual report and statement of accounts — 73-644668 — #1787528
12. Mining Symposium. Annual Mining Symposium — 48-36897 — #9616899
13. New England economic almanac — sf88-91109 — #7104447
14. General embryological information service — sn83-10929 — #1779150
15. OECD financial statistics — 78-642704 — #1841149
16. The Nursing journals index — 83-644137 — #9635534
17. Quarterly economic review of China, North Korea — 82-647227 — #8277176
18. American men of science — 06-7326 — #1354617
19. The American philatelist — 08-22708 — #1480549
20. Angewandte Chemie (Weinheim an der Bergstrasse, Germany) — 13-3396 — #5845277
21. Environmental science & technology — 68-5797 — #1568096

22.	ABMEES	82-646096	#7140542
23.	Annual bulletin (International Dairy Federation)	sn94-15507	#1753497
24.	Industrial diamond review	56-2274	#1645049
25.	Dalīl al-kitāb al-Misrī	72-960043	#3799080
26.	Archives de philosophie	84-641660	#1772219
27.	Review of scientific instruments	32-17560	#1763839
28.	Analytical chemistry	31-21682	#1481078

NAMED SUPPLEMENTS NOT PUBLISHED SEPARATELY

1.	Corail (Noumea, New Caledonia : 1980)	sn82-21410	#7493588
2.	French studies	52-52554	#1242098
3.	3-trend security charts	73-640821	#6180538
4.	United States. President. Economic report of the President transmitted to the Congress	47-32975	#1193149
5.	Encyclopedia of American associations	59-6963	#1223565
6.	Center for Creative Photography (Series)	sf88-19518	#3338330
7.	SIGBIO newsletter of the Association for Computing Machinery Special Interest Group on Biomedical Computing	92-642728	#4411991
8.	Review of scientific instruments	32-17560	#1763839

SPECIAL ISSUES

1.	JEI report	sn82-20877	#7077306
2.	Abstract bibliography on coconut		#9424063
3.	International journal of physical distribution and materials management	82-646080	#3760812
4.	Evaluation and change	sc82-8179	#6504146
5.	Landscape & turf industry	82-646507	#6441588
6.	Classical Association of Canada. Canadian classical bulletin		#35923809

UPDATES

1.	Book publishers directory	82-640252	#3231742
2.	Guide to U.S. Government publications	74-646648	#1795366
3.	Directory of corporate affiliations	83-641510	#1221072
4.	Directory of corporate affiliations of major corporations	83-641774	#1221060
5.	Physicians' desk reference	82-642489	#1311259
6.	United States. Federal Aviation Administration. Federal aviation regulations. Part 39, Airworthiness directives	81-640689	#4021147

7. Exporters' encyclopaedia. World marketing guide — 82-641772 — #6138540
8. Habitat preservation abstracts — sn86-44018 — #6676478
9. Handbook of accounting and auditing — sn83-10351 — #7756639
10. Gazetteer of Canada — 55-15326 — #2627395
11. International marketing handbook — 88-647663 — #8119702
12. Commission of the European Communities. Library (Brussels, Belgium). EF-publikationer og dokumenter modtaget af biblioteket — 86-650558 — #13695412

ACCOMPANYING INFORMATION

1. Alinorm — 81-649265 — #1650325
2. International Joint Commission. Biennial report under the Great Lakes Water Quality Agreement of 1978 — 83-643527 — #9025749
3. Health manpower provincial report, Manitoba — 76-642439 — #2580880
4. United States. Dept. of the Interior National Park System new area studies, threatened natural landmarks and nationally significant historic places — 83-642416 — #5869414
5. Equal employment opportunity in the federal courts — 82-646840 — #8506032
6. Flood control project maintenance and repair . . . inspection report — 79-644725 — #5762082
7. Flood control project maintenance and repair . . . inspection report — 79-644725 — #5762082
8. Flue — sc82-4472 — #8150495
9. Physics of the earth and planetary interiors — sf80-1253 — #878793
10. IEEE transactions on education — 64-974 — #1752549

530 ADDITIONAL PHYSICAL FORM AVAILABLE NOTE

1. IEE proceedings. G, Electronic circuits and systems — 82-643911 — #6046660
2. Nuclear technology/fusion — 81-641143 — #6831387
3. Advances in space research — 83-645550 — #7004415
4. The Journal for special educators — 80-644999 — #4409595
5. Journal of experimental psychology. Human learning and memory — 76-643081 — #1172614
6. Library of Congress. Subject headings in microform — 79-641066 — #3454199

7.	Computational linguistics (Association for Computational Linguistics)	88-654977	#11322424
8.	Employment fact book for the period . . .	80-648102	#6522950
9.	Community services catalyst (Remote access)		#31494925
10.	Apicultural information and issues (Online)	95-647858	#32207891
11.	Wilson applied science & technology abstracts	96-647356	#30578340
12.	JAIR	sn95-35410	#32636311
13.	Postmodern culture	sn90-3259	#22471982
14.	Entertainment magazine on-line	sn96-184	#34522805
15.	Emerging infectious diseases (Online)	sn95-7042	#31848943
16.	United States. Supreme Court. Cases argued and decided in the Supreme Court of the United States	86-645603	#13941398
17.	United States. Supreme Court. U.S. Supreme Court reports, L Ed	sn97-32827	#36236579
18.	Architectural publications index on disc	sn96-23120	#33072688
19.	Flora online (Computer disk ed.)	sn88-28171	#17217968
20.	Cambridge structural database system	sn96-47038	#34331851
21.	Direction of trade statistics	81-649851	#7154584

533 REPRODUCTION NOTE

1.	The Reporter for conscience' sake	sc83-9165	#4531001
2.	Statisticheski godishnik na Narodna Republika Bŭlgariâ	sc82-8195	#8776525
3.	VocEd	sc82-7260	#4650443

534 ORIGINAL VERSION NOTE

Examples taken from *CONSER Editing Guide*, 1994 ed.

535 LOCATION OF ORIGINALS/DUPLICATES NOTE

Examples taken from *CONSER Editing Guide*, 1994 ed.

538 SYSTEM DETAILS NOTE

SYSTEM REQUIREMENTS

1.	Compact disc Code of Federal Regulations. E, H & S updated as of . . .	95-645829	#33097541

2.	Scientific American medicine (CD-ROM)	sn94-30519	#28898230
3.	Opal dictionary of occupational titles	95-641378	#32176479
4.	Eurocat	sn94-30177	#30346682
5.	Hua-hsia wen chai	sn95-42471	#33397925

MODE OF ACCESS

1.	The computists' communique	sn95-6170	#32986585
2.	Journal of political economy (Online)	sn97-23016	#35738289
3.	CONSER Program. CONSERline	95-647859	#29049140
4.	Current cites	sn91-7993	#24894089
5.	Disaster research		#31494529
6.	Disaster research		#31494529
7.	DLA bulletin (Electronic version)	sn94-3597	#29905912

VIDEORECORDINGS

Examples taken from *CONSER Editing Guide*, 1994 ed.

546 LANGUAGE NOTE

LANGUAGE OF TEXT

1.	Pharmatherapeutica	sn82-4598	#2145498
2.	Library of Congress. Library of Congress Office, New Delhi. Accessions list, South Asia	sc83-3005	#8961462
3.	The China phone book & address directory	90-656195	#4011437
4.	Orient (Deutsches Orient-Institut)	83-644299	#2679292
5.	Anuário estatístico (Macao. Repartição dos Serviços de Estatística)	83-642844	#5041852
6.	Bulletin trimestriel de la Société belge de photogrammétrie et de télédétection	82-643582	#8351882
7.	Canadian review of physical anthropology	cn80-30468	#6244471
8.	The Tax/benefit position of selected income groups in OECD member countries	sc82-7588	#7208615
9.	Acadiensis	92-641132	#1670823
10.	Studi germanici	82-646613	#1766653
11.	Manitoba modern language journal	cn83-30181	#9414391
12.	Boerhaave cahiers	sc82-5046	#8416588
13.	Argile	sc83-6089	#1268486
14.	Canada. Dept. of Fisheries and Oceans. Report of operations under the	81-645480	#7805054

	Fisheries Development Act for the fiscal year ended Mar. 31 . . .		
15.	Canada. Transport Canada. Annual report	83-643545	#8714973
16.	Bundesanstalt für Geowissenschaften und Rohstoffe. Tätigkeitsbericht - Bundesanstalt für Geowissenschaften und Rohstoffe	76-648862	#2767029
17.	Government of Canada internal energy conservation program	80-640412	#5018287
18.	Newsletter (International Centre for the Study of the Preservation and the Restoration of Cultural Property)	92-642742	#6624877
19.	Eurocat	sn94-30177	#30346682
20.	SCAD+CD	sn96-31505	#28614306
21.	Vlaamse centrale catalogus op cd-rom	95-652165	#33039934
22.	from *CONSER Editing Guide,* 1994 ed.		

LANGUAGE OF SUMMARY, ETC.

1.	Anurio (Instituto Boliviano de Biología de Altura)	82-643788	#8539728
2.	Abhandlungen des Naturwissenschaftlichen Vereins in Hamburg	sn82-309	#7547018
3.	Acta Universitatis Lodziensis. Folia sociologica	89-640080	#8125367
4.	Chūgoku gogaku	84-640440	#3134171
5.	Kontakt (Paris, France)	83-644172	#9492349
6.	Avian pathology	sc83-2184	#2199397
7.	Gedrag	83-642254	#1185079
8.	Gelişme dergisi	85-649468	#5583278
9.	Annales de microbiologic. B		#2257525
10.	Acta medica iranica	sn79-5711	#1460918
11.	Les Carnets de l'enfance	68-348	#1241999
12.	Garcia de Orta	58-20407	#1570413
13.	Neophilologica	82-641207	#7937380
14.	Akita igaku	sc83-2756	#8742651
15.	International journal of sport psychology	82-646974	#1753592
16.	Zoologische Jahrbücher. Abteilung für Anatomie und Ontogenie der Tiere	82-645526	#1645063
17.	Jugoslavenska akademija znanosti I umjetnosti. Institut u Zadru. Radovi	58-20476	#1782815
18.	Sweden. Postverket	78-642683	#3108753

TRANSLATION INFORMATION

1. Revista nacional de telecomunicações   82-643575   #8072118
   (International edition)
2. Tradition médicale chinoise   sc82-5262   #8653846
3. Artful dodge   sn80-134   #5872806

547 FORMER TITLE COMPLEXITY NOTE

Examples taken from *CONSER Editing Guide*, 1994 ed.

550 ISSUING BODY NOTE

GENERAL ISSUING BODY NOTES

1.	Checklist of official Pennsylvania publications	82-641505	#2259176
2.	Detailed mortality statistics, Alabama	82-643453	#5719288
3.	Current industrial reports. ITA-9008, Copper controlled materials	80-644856	#4506691
4.	Encuesta nacional de bovinos, X región, prov. Osorno	82-643772	#8537543
5.	Control of Power Systems Conference & Exposition. Conference record	82-642090	#3597953
6.	EACROTANAL information	sc83-6382	#8333682
7.	Current issue outline	82-645448	#6492410
8.	British Crop Protection Conference—Weeds. Proceedings of the British Crop Protection Conference—Weeds	sn80-13359	#3949267
9.	Audiovisual materials	80-648903	#4782873
10.	Annual report to the legislature on the mandatory vehicle inspection program (MVIP)	sc83-1150	#9013972
11.	Gulf Coast Association of Geological Societies. Transactions	52-24459	#7887134
12.	Pacific review (San Diego, Calif.)	83-647093	#9834503
13.	Australian journal of developmental disabilities	sn81-4344	#6720282
14.	Geological Survey (U.S.). Water Resources Division. Ground-water levels in observation wells in Arkansas	82-647378	#9086425
15.	Labour arbitration cases, 3rd ser.	sn82-22122	#8103793
16.	Agricultural finance outlook	80-644040	#5791912
17.	Configurations (Online)	sn95-7065	#31870355
18.	Community services catalyst (Remote access)		#31494925

19.	New horizons in adult education	sn92-4590	#23865312
20.	Physicians' SilverPlatter. Cardiology	94-646720	#30885735
21.	Wasteinfo	94-660774	#30786474

PUBLISHER INFORMATION

1.	Evaluation and change	sc82-8179	#6504146
2.	Asian outlook	65-9952	#1514436
3.	Onomastica Slavogermanica	a66-279	#5912743
4.	Inter-American music bulletin	pa57-186	#1588355
5.	Alcheringa (New York, N.Y.)	72-626511	#1780749
6.	Annual review of jazz studies	82-644466	#8099505
7.	German chemical engineering	sn82-20491	#4441440
8.	Information series (Colorado Geological Survey)	sf82-3133	#2129065
9.	International journal of hospitality management	82-643994	#7827955
10.	The Stalnaker chronicles	84-642804	#10729656
11.	Advances in test anxiety research	83-640266	#9135225
12.	Oxford journal of legal studies	83-645842	#7636038

OFFICIAL ORGAN, PUBLICATION, ETC.

1.	Forest industries (Auckland, N.Z.)	sc82-4222	#8101814
2.	Africa calls from Rhodesia	sf82-3147	#8754333
3.	Improving human performance quarterly	sc78-82	#2921859
4.	Annales de géographie	sn79-9782	#3341949
5.	The computists' communique	sn95-6170	#32986585

VARIANT NAMES

1.	U.S. directory of environmental sources	sn79-5033	#5052744
2.	Health manpower provincial report, Manitoba	76-642439	#2580880
3.	Technical report (Skipjack Survey and Assessment Programme)	sn83-10411	#8541060
4.	Law and politics book review	95-660724	#25724298

555 CUMULATIVE INDEX/FINDING AIDS NOTE

FORMAL NOTES

1.	Bulletin (Columbia Society of International Law)	97-660536	#3529661
2.	The Journal of law and economic development	sn83-3988	#9244370

3.	American Oriental Society. Journal of the American Oriental Society	12-32032	#1480509
4.	Blake	78-642274	#3160132
5.	Biological reviews and biological proceedings of the Cambridge Philosophical Society	sf84-8007	#3674460
6.	The Harvard International Law Club bulletin	sf87-92681	#7898463
7.	Zapiski Rossiĭskogo mineralogicheskogo obshchestva	sf83-5009	#8426157
8.	Hanging loose	83-640340	#1877219
9.	Science of religion bulletin	sn82-21840	#7473942
10.	Industrial diamond abstracts	56-2274	#1645049

INFORMAL NOTES

1.	Annales de geographic	sn79-9782	#3341949
2.	Food & nutrition	73-649337	#7081733
3.	Biochemistry abstracts. Part 1, Biological membranes	sc82-7512	#6001716
4.	Bulletin of prosthetics research	sn84-11428	#1537770
5.	Journal of marketing research	sc82-4518	#3808338
6.	Progress in inorganic chemistry	59-13035	#1645674
7.	Great Britain. Parliament. House of Commons. Parliamentary debates (Hansard). House of Commons official report	10-3568	#8985610
8.	Moccasin telegraph (Ottawa, Ont.)	cn81-311099	#2068331
9.	The Menges Family Association in America	83-643951	#9599842
10.	New special libraries	sn79-7093	#4069542
11.	American Society for Testing and Materials. Annual book of ASTM standards	83-641658	#2187052
12.	Resources in education	75-644211	#2241688
13.	Inland bird banding	82-647359	#5055631
14.	Nordicom. Bibliography of Nordic mass communications literature	79-646477	#4030466
15.	Federal evaluations	82-640705	#7018279
16.	USAPAT	96-660804	#31190600

556 INFORMATION ABOUT DOCUMENTATION NOTE

1.	Moody's international annual reports	sn96-380139	#34948695
2.	Ethics index	95-660988	#33322402
3.	APSRS	sn95-20078	#32315307

4.	Opal United States immigration law library	95-645695	#32210991
5.	Artikelbasen	sn96-32079	#33670510
6.	Cetedoc library of Christian Latin texts	sn95-43285	#31595588
7.	Electronic clipper	96-647358	#34187454
8.	Agrostate-PC. Trade	sn95-43279	#32324922

580 LINKING ENTRY COMPLEXITY NOTE

ORIGINAL LANGUAGE

1.	Problems of the Far East		#4990413
2.	Cofiec. Cofiec annual report	74-648118	#1796320
3.	Biologia medica (Istituto nazionale di chemioterapia (Italy))	sc82-2494	#8653221
4.	Mechanical sciences - mashinovedenie	73-647778	#1789806
5.	Mechanical sciences abstracts	73-647776	#1789805

TRANSLATION

1.	Mashinovedenie	90-646274	#6258868
2.	Mashinovedenie	90-646274	#6258868

SUPPLEMENT/SPECIAL ISSUE

1.	Directory of corporate affiliations	83-641510	#1221072
2.	Gazette des beaux-arts	08-18272	#1570479
3.	The Journal of the Acoustical Society of America	sn78-654	#1226792
4.	Standard & Poor's creditweek	82-640380	#7910037
5.	World agriculture outlook & situation	82-645566	#7746750
6.	Stata	sn96-47867	#35648344
7.	Survey of current business	21-26819	#1697070
8.	Medical subject headings. Annotated alphabetic list	80-644513	#6392946
9.	Merchant marine examination questions. Book 3, Nav. general	sn93-27690	#28003906
10.	Science world	sn81-424	#7142779
11.	International labour review	sn83-4074	#5345843
12.	The Auk	sf79-10123	#1518634
13.	Notices of the American Mathematical Society	sf77-404	#1480366
14.	The Floating bear	74-648009	#3704931
15.	Datapro directory of small computers	sn81-4234	#7332427
16.	Back stage	sn78-1204	#1519001

PARENT RECORD

1.	Outlook (Philadelphia, Pa.)	82-647121	#8508874
2.	Euromoney five hundred	82-646470	#8585694
3.	Public Relations Society of America. PRSA directory	sn83-10568	#7781945
4.	Nature. Directory of biologicals	82-647157	#8042438
5.	Business screen (New York, N.Y.)	82-644834	#7356032
6.	Techniques (Saint-Étienne (Loire, France))	sn82-20428	#6400380
7.	IBRO news	83-646493	#2001973
8.	State legislative leadership, committees, and staff	79-644269	#5123302
9.	Industrial diamond review	56-2274	#1645049
10.	Recent literature	sn85-61142	#4303052
11.	Instrument manufacturing. The . . . buyers' guide	46-5138	#8816047
12.	Directory information service	77-641771	#3208182
13.	European brokers survey	95-648172	#32082474
14.	Cerrahpaşa medical review	sc83-4105	#8983811
15.	Mini-annals of improbable research	sn94-5215	#30496676
16.	Pressdok	sn91-28014	#23132733
17.	Corporate giving watch	sc82-7555	#8123791
18.	Ohio official reports (Cincinnati, Ohio : Advance sheets)	sn82-5967	#8610029
19.	Merchant marine examination questions. New & revised engineering questions	sn94-28521	#31243867
20.	Social security bulletin. Annual statistical supplement	sc77-385	#1939422
21.	Advertising age. 100 leading markets	sc84-1229	#10249335
22.	Direction of trade statistics. Yearbook	82-646788	#7866916

OTHER EDITION AVAILABLE

A. General

1.	English journal	14-13041	#1325886
2.	Lancet (London, England)	sf82-2015	#1755507
3.	Geo (Dee Why West, A.C.T.)	90-640416	#7618351
4.	Information industry market place	81-643678	#7004484
5.	Orpheus (London, England : 1948)	48-21925	#4250720
6.	U.S. information Moscow	sc82-4485	#8067779

B. Other language editions

1.	Présence africaine	51-31032	#1639236
2.	Meridiane 12-23	sc82-5224	#8692536

3.	Telcom report	81-644095	#4326720
4.	Āfāq (Giv{c}at Havivah, Israel)	83-642884	#9449680
5.	Canadian Nuclear Society. Conference. Transactions	81-645711	#7802485
6.	Advertising age.	42-47059	#1461285
7.	Esquire (New York, N.Y.)	82-647273	#5154955
8.	Finance & development	75-648861	# 2246726

C. Reprint editions

1.	Armchair detective	82-643921	#8556372
2.	Colónida	82-647145	#9055962
3.	Nosotros (Mexico City, Mexico : 1912)	83-643751	#7918686
4.	La Falange	81-646413	#6912976
5.	Dav	82-644154	#6204769
6.	Ulises (Mexico City, Mexico)	82-643062	#7918688
7.	Locus	78-648218	#4386151
8.	The Floating bear	74-648009	#3704931
9.	Gazette des beaux-arts	80-649794	#7119790
10.	China. Chien she wei yüan hui. Chien she wei yüan hui kung pao	82-642240	#8996074
11.	Owari no iseki to ibutsu	83-643221	#9503794
12.	Arxiu de tradicions populars recollides a Catalunya, Valencia, Mallorca, Rosselló, Sardenya, Andorra I terres aragoneses de parla catalana	80-649045	#6839654
13.	Art in America. Annual guide to galleries, museums, artists	83-640849	#9179141

ISSUED WITH

A. Issued with

1.	Association for Childhood Education International. ACEI exchange	82-642762	#8229035
2.	Legal times of Washington (1982)	82-643347	#8239960
3.	GT guide to world equity markets	91-658525	#15254771
4.	Studies in American Jewish literature	77-649500	#2747242
5.	American Association of Housing Educators. Conference. Proceedings of the . . . annual conference	82-646586	#8446286
6.	Bibliography of Asian studies	73-617426	#4285212
7.	Barron's index	76-640128	#1984310
8.	Bulletin (Institution of Mining and Metallurgy (Great Britain))	49-51907	#2765082
9.	Proceedings (American Society of Civil Engineers)	06-9456	#1480784
10.	Religion in America	sn83-10128	#6745609

11.	Gallup report (Princeton, N.J. : 1981)	83-643597	#7543533
12.	Chemistry (Weinheim an der Bergstrasse, Germany)	sn95-26440	#32677914
13.	American choral review	sn78-421	#1479659
14.	Garden design	82-647188	#8610163
15.	Computing reviews	66-98189	#1564620

B. "Includes" statements

1.	Transactions. Section C, Mineral processing & extractive metallurgy	sc82-7357	#2401167
2.	Outlook (Palo Alto, Calif.)	81-642508	#6878240
3.	United States pharmacopeia	83-640088	#5623396
4.	Biblica	32-12677	#1519715
5.	Metals and materials	sn82-22249	#1757192
6.	Journal of Asian studies	sn83-7017	#1713826
7.	Annales de géographie	sn79-9782	#3341949
8.	Designers West	81-641142	#4087182
9.	Illinois. Dept. of Mines and Minerals. Coal report of Illinois	sc80-1080	#2371496
10.	Harris Ohio marketers industrial directory: MID	82-644198	#8021765
11.	Drug, the nurse, the patient	66-15620	#3995456
12.	Current drug handbook	58-6390	#1565622
13.	Current anthropology	a63-576	#1565600
14.	Voice of Chorus America	95-640195	#24620697
15.	Childhood education	26-4861	#1554226

PRECEDING TITLE

A. Continuations

1.	Acta embryologiae et morphologiae experimentalis ("Halocynthia" Association)	sc82-7167	#7302987
2.	Corail (Noumea, New Caledonia : 1980)	sn82-21410	#7493588
3.	American Society of Civil Engineers. Water Resources Planning and Management Division. Journal of the Water Resources Planning and Management Division	76-645470	#2200366
4.	National accounts statistics. Main aggregates and detailed tables	86-647250	#12148091
5.	Carnets de l'enfance	68-348	#1241999
6.	Annual energy outlook	83-645822	#9587622
7.	Hospital statistics (American Hospital Association)	72-626765	#1689227
8.	Index chemicus (Philadelphia, Pa. : 1977)	83-642297	#3024693

9. Balance of payments statistics	sc82-7397	#7154626
10. Martindale-Hubbell international law directory	91-649724	#23266418
11. Directory of auto supply chains	82-643079	#7979782
12. Schweisstechnik	58-46242	#7102106
13. Industrial wastes (Chicago, Ill. : 1971)	82-646131	#2038241
14. Funde und Ausgrabungen im Bezirk Trier	sc83-5046	#8966929
15. Martindale-Hubbell international law digest	96-660611	#27396188
16. National Association of Retail Druggists. N.A.R.D. newsletter	78-645112	#4102933
17. City government finances in . . .	74-648912	#1796776
18. International energy outlook	86-650629	#13696840
19. Brookings papers on economic activity. Microeconomics	89-640223	#19985852

B. Continuations in different formats

1. Communication world (San Francisco, Calif. : 1983)	sn85-11887	#10897719
2. Energy statistics handbook (Diskette)	sn96-32750	#35709875
3. Research, scholarship, creative and performing art (Windows version)	96-660501	#34051323
4. Lighthouse electronic magazine	sn96-3885	#34074466
5. Industry review (Diskette)	sn96-38129	#35111416
6. Index translationum (CD-ROM)	95-660578	#32027032

C. Mergers or unions

1. New scientist and science journal	82-644453	#2378327
2. IEE proceedings. G, Electronic circuits and systems	82-643911	#6046660
3. Monthly vital statistics report (Hyattsville, Md.)	66-51898	#1685363
4. Acta botanica Barcinonensia	sn82-20968	#4533507
5. Artikelbasen	sn96-32079	#33670510

D. Absorptions

1. Forthcoming books	67-1000	#1569855
2. Childhood education	26-4861	#1554226
3. Industrial diamond review	56-2274	#1645049
4. American municipal news	68-1596	#4737190
5. Nuclear instruments & methods in physics research	81-643559	#7608866

SUCCEEDING TITLE

A. Continuations

1.	World agriculture outlook & situation	82-645566	#7746750
2.	Journal of geophysical research. Oceans and atmospheres	83-641460	#3918273
3.	Current abstracts of chemistry and index chemicus	76-613303	#2112946
4.	High fidelity (Musical America ed. : 1980)	83-640343	#7081128
5.	Monthly bibliography of medical reviews	sc78-2150	#1768569
6.	Journal of materials science	78-211246	#1754660
7.	American Society of Heating, Refrigerating and Air-Conditioning Engineers. ASHRAE handbook & product directory	73-644272	#1787246
8.	Hospitals (Chicago, Ill. : 1936)	43-4821	#1752305
9.	National Association of Retail Druggists. N.A.R.D. journal	80-644613	#1695474
10.	OLPR bulletin	sc81-3133	#2251560
11.	Technik	49-4151	#2058956
12.	United States. Energy Information. Administration. Annual report to Congress	78-643480	#3793497
13.	Annual energy outlook	83-645822	#9587622
14.	Water & sewage works	34-19619	#1769488

B. Continuations in different formats

1.	Index translationum	50-12446	#2433763
2.	Research report - Monash University	76-642337	#2376437
3.	Energy statistics handbook	92-64132	#25796851
4.	Value line industry review	sn92-17175	#24916684

C. Mergers

1.	IEE proceedings. G, Electronic circuits and systems	82-643911	#6046660
2.	Business Mexico	90-661033	#10535093
3.	Liebigs Annalen der Chemie	80-644142	#4719928
4.	Dansk artikelindeks	sc82-3322	#8325590
5.	India news (Washington, D.C. : 1956)	sn79-7192	#2447545

D. Absorptions

1.	Association for Childhood Education International. ACEI exchange	82-642762	#8229035
2.	Scott chronicle of new issues	sn83-7211	#8981078

3. American municipal news	68-1596	#4737190
4. Federal Reserve Bank of Philadelphia. Annual report	18-26424	#1295599

E. Splits

1. Balance of payments yearbook	sn82-21742	#1425761
2. American Society of Heating, Refrigerating and Air-Conditioning Engineers. ASHRAE handbook & product directory.	73-644272	#1787246
3. Garcia de Orta	58-20407	#1570413
4. Comptes rendus des séances de l'Académie des sciences. Vie académique	81-642839	#7029828
5. Carnets de l'enfance. Assignment children	1241999	#1241999

NONSPECIFIC RELATIONSHIP

A. Shared contents

1. World*data	sn95-43275	#32035140
2. Arctic & antarctic regions	92-644419	#19545098
3. Million dollar disc	92-660656	#22038744
4. TreeCD	sn95-43801	#28613563
5. Variety's video directory plus	92-646052	#26231669
6. Encyclopedia of associations (Online)	sn96-34036	#34147706
7. American men & women of science	89-645423	#19407934
8. Books in print	74-643574	#1641212
9. Judicial staff directory	87-640790	#13238092
10. Washington State vital statistics (Olympia, Wash. : 1994)	sn95-43481	#32062454

B. Previous publication

1. Quarterly coal report (United States. Energy Information Administration. Office of Coal, Nuclear, Electric, and Alternate Fuels)	sc83-1108	#8911051
2. Felt and damaging earthquakes	83-644775	#6440198
3. Bulletin of labour statistics	166-263	#1537758
4. Geochemistry (Chung-kuo k^{c}uang wu yen shih ti ch^{c}iu hua hsüeh hsüeh hui)	83-642398	#8618622
5. Survey of current business	21-26819	#1697070
6. Engineering index . . . subject index	sn88-273	#17418862
7. Engineering index annual	83-644622	#5118578
8. Mémoires de la Société fribourgeoise des sciences naturelles. Géologie et géographie	sf83-9037	#1716293

9.	Annual of American architecture	81-640394	#7082973
10.	Trends and perspectives in parasitology	81-642963	#7654173
11.	Readings in Gulf Coast geology	sn82-7438	#7378726
12.	Gulf Coast Association of Geological Societies. Transactions	52-24459	#7887134
13.	Americana (New York, N.Y.: 1925)	25-23066	#2923293
14.	American Heart Association monograph	sf81-1017	#1695120

C. Issued as

1.	Nursing job news nursing job guide to over 7,000 hospitals	sn79-4698	#4252505
2.	Federal Deposit Insurance Corporation. Annual report	sc83-7079	#9094778
3.	American Mathematical Society. List of officers and members	13-24071	#5586858
4.	Theochem	82-641126	#7073454
5.	American perfumer and aromatics	sc78-785	#2630124
6.	Journal of molecular structure	sf78-588	#1136815
7.	Annual report on carcinogens	80-647787	#6543913

D. Cumulations, compilations, summaries

1.	Deutsche Bibliographie Wöchentliches Verzeichnis	87-642473	#15330261
2.	Bibliography of agriculture (National Agricultural Library (U.S.) : 1980)	85-645975	#7896413
3.	F&S index Europe (Foster City, Calif.)	sf94-34006	#28315880
4.	Survey of current business	21-26819	#1697070
5.	Water resources data for Colorado	68-60770	#1159412
6.	Advance data from Vital & health statistics of the National Center for Health Statistics	79-643688	#2778178
7.	Serials in the British Library (Annual)	sn84-10171	#8264921
8.	Survey of current business (CD-ROM version)	95-655290	#32717486
9.	Deutsche Bibliographie. Halbjahres-Verzeichnis	52-39843	#5816404
10.	F&S index United States annual	94-657040	#29994936
11.	Physical education index (Annual)	82-644892	#7890091
12.	Joint acquisitions list of Africana (Annual cumulation)	84-647202	#6654709
13.	Index medicus (National Library of Medicine (U.S.))	61-60337	#1752728
14.	Engineering index annual	83-644622	#5118578
15.	Audiovisual materials	80-648903	#4782873

16.	Annual insider index to public policy studies	83-644562	#9212455
17.	Insider newsletter	sc85-8097	#11130031
18.	Journal of taxation digest	84-649797	#8059457
19.	Los Angeles County wage and salary and civilian labor force employment estimate	sc83-7706	#9870778
20.	International marketing handbook	sn82-6673	#8119702
21.	Biogenic amines and transmitters in the nervous system	sc79-4875	#4939815

E. Updates

1.	America buys	81-642345	#6559169
2.	Law . . . information	83-643008	#9151843
3.	Books in print	74-643574	#1641212
4.	Books in print supplement	80-647662	#2429038
5.	Forthcoming books	67-1000	#1569855

F. Indexes

1.	Name of applicants for the registration of trade marks	82-641867	#8289687
2.	Government reports annual index	76-648535	#1781413
3.	Curriculum development library. Cumulative index	sn83-10187	#6677031
4.	Index of mathematical papers	72-624335	#1752735
5.	Government reports announcements & index	75-645021	#2242215
6.	INFO-LEX. Skorowidz obowiązujących przepisów prawnych	93-648945	#29205779
7.	Books in print	sf90-90146	#8456640
8.	Books in print	74-643574	#1641212
9.	Subject guide to Books in print	74-643573	#1641085

G. Companion publications

1.	Medical subject headings. Annotated alphabetic list	80-644513	#6392946
2.	Typological studies in language	sn84-10367	#10388792
3.	POLP ASIST	sn91-19569	#24675059
4.	Magazine index plus	sn94-15265	#31619759
5.	Hospital statistics (American Hospital Association)	72-626765	#1689227
6.	Journal of materials science	78-211246	#1754660
7.	Applied physics letters	64-6603	#1580952
8.	Reverse acronyms, initialisms, & abbreviations dictionary	sn80-13153	#4416864

9.	Variety (New York, N.Y.)	ca07-4418	#1768958
10.	Arquitectura (Mexico City, Mexico : 1991)	93-655695	#28740154
11.	Foundation directory	60-13807	#918159
12.	MLA directory of periodicals: a guide to journals and series in languages and literatures	80-640485	#5350432
13.	Scott stamp monthly	8932842	#8932842
14.	Bulletin of labour statistics	l66-263	#1537758
15.	Peterson's study abroad	94-664121	#28130277
16.	Annual energy outlook	83-645822	#9587622

H. Miscellaneous nonspecific relationships

1.	Conference on Modern Jewish Studies. Conference on Modern Jewish Studies annual	80-644319	#3580537
2.	New car yearbook	94-642313	#30629172
3.	Annual energy outlook	83-645822	#9587622
4.	America's best graduate schools	95-644336	#23660464
5.	Atlantic Provinces Linguistic Association. Meeting. Papers from the . . . annual meeting of the Atlantic Provinces Linguistics Association	82-640192	#7857905
6.	Beiträge zur Geschichte der deutschen Sprache und Literatur	57-22131	#1519380
7.	Beiträge zur Geschichte der deutschen Sprache und Literatur	01-16684	#1587656
8.	Bulletin of Hispanic studies	34-16561	#4900237
9.	Bulletin of Hispanic studies (Liverpool, England : 1996)	sn97-30969	#36752298
10.	Bryn Mawr reviews	sn93-2792	#28523082
11.	Histoire littéraire du Québec	83-642183	#7669552
12.	Franchise opportunities	86-640031	#7579012
13.	Antitrust law & economics review	sf76-119	#1481629

I. Related non-serial publications

1.	Personal property security act cases	83-645286	#9046972
2.	Writings on American history	04-8590	#1770230
3.	Biographical directory of the American Congress	sn96-4786	#35646120
4.	Introductory bibliography for Japanese studies	92-644947	#5421473
5.	Current facts	sn96-47022	#25597220
6.	Readers' guide to periodical literature (Cumulative volume)	06-8232	#5855603

WORKS CONSULTED AND CITED

CONSER Editing Guide. 1994 ed. Washington, DC: Library of Congress, Serial Record Division, 1994.

Format Integration and Its Effect on the USMARC Bibliographic Format. 1995 ed. Washington, DC: Library of Congress, Cataloging Distribution Service, 1995.

Hirons, Jean L., ed. *CONSER Cataloging Manual.* Washington, DC: Library of Congress, Serial Record Division, 1993.

OCLC Bibliographic Formats and Standards. 2nd ed. Dublin, OH: OCLC, 1996.

SUGGESTED READINGS

Blixrud, Julia C. *A Manual of AACR2 Examples for Serials*. 2nd ed. Lake Crystal, MN: Soldier Creek Press, 1988.

Cannan, Judith Proctor. *Special Problems in Serials Cataloging*. Washington, DC: Library of Congress, 1979.

Cataloging & Classification Quarterly. Vol. 1, no. 1- . New York: Haworth Press, 1980- .

Cataloging Service Bulletin. No. 1- . Washington, DC: Library of Congress, 1978- .

CONSER Editing Guide. 1994 ed. Washington, DC: Library of Congress, Serial Record Division, 1994.

Edgar, Neal L., ed. *AACR2 and Serials: The American View*. New York: Haworth Press, 1983.

Hirons, Jean L., ed. *CONSER Cataloging Manual*. Washington, DC: Library of Congress, Serial Record Division, 1993.

Osborn, Andrew Delbridge. *Serial Publications, Their Place and Treatment in Libraries*. 3rd ed. Chicago: American Library Association, 1980.

Serials Librarian. Vol. 1, no. 1- . New York: Haworth Press, 1976- .

Serials Review. Vol. 1, no. 1- . Ann Arbor, MI: Pierian Press, 1975- .

Smith, Lynn S. *A Practical Approach to Serials Cataloging*. Greenwich, CT: JAI Press, 1978.

Taylor, Arlene G., and Bohdan S. Wynar. *Introduction to Cataloging and Classification*. 8th ed. Englewood, CO: Libraries Unlimited, 1992.

Tuttle, Marcia. *Managing Serials*. Greenwich, CT: JAI Press, 1996.

Index

This index lists concepts rather than simple terms, as the following example illustrates: The concept of "inclusion" refers to bibliographic relationships. Therefore, you will find a reference under the index entry " 'Includes' statements" to the note, "*Includes* a separately numbered title: Monthly statement," but not to the note, "Number of each issue *includes* initials of agency." For ease of use, the index provides several inverted terms and grammatical variations. Reference is to page number.